NOT EVEN PAST

≋

LAWRENCE STONE LECTURES
Sponsored by
The Shelby Cullom Davis Center for Historical Studies
and Princeton University Press
2009

PREVIOUS LAWRENCE STONE LECTURES

Mark Mazower, *No Enchanted Palace:*
The End of Empire and the Ideological Origins of the United Nations

NOT EVEN PAST

≋

Barack Obama and the Burden of Race

THOMAS J. SUGRUE

PRINCETON UNIVERSITY PRESS

PRINCETON AND OXFORD

Published by Princeton University Press, 41 William Street,
Princeton, New Jersey 08540

In the United Kingdom: Princeton University Press, 6 Oxford Street,
Woodstock, Oxfordshire OX20 1TW
press.princeton.edu

LIBRARY OF CONGRESS CATALOGING-IN-PUBLICATION DATA
Sugrue, Thomas J., 1962–
Not even past : Barack Obama and the burden of race / Thomas J. Sugrue.
p. cm. — (Lawrence Stone lectures)
Includes bibliographical references.
ISBN 978-0-691-13730-8 (hardcover : alk. paper)
1. Obama, Barack. 2. Obama, Barack—Political and social views.
3. African Americans—Race identity. 4. Presidents—United States—
Biography. 5. African Americans—Biography.
6. African Americans—Civil rights. 7. United States—
Race relations—Political aspects. 8. Racism—Political aspects—
United States. 9. Social classes—Political aspects—United States.
10. Political culture—United States. I. Title.
E908.3.S84 2010
973.932092—dc22   2010000240

British Library Cataloging-in-Publication Data is available

This book has been composed in Sabon
Printed on acid-free paper. ∞
Printed in the United States of America

1 3 5 7 9 10 8 6 4 2

To MBK

The past is not dead. In fact, it's not even past.
—*William Faulkner, Requiem for a Nun*

As William Faulkner once wrote, "The past isn't dead and buried. In fact, it isn't even past." We do not need to recite here the history of racial injustice in this country. But we do need to remind ourselves that so many of the disparities that exist in the African-American community today can be directly traced to inequalities passed on from an earlier generation that suffered under the brutal legacy of slavery and Jim Crow.
—*Barack Obama, "A More Perfect Union," Philadelphia, March 18, 2008*

≡

Contents

≣

NOT EVEN PAST

≋

Introduction

≋

It is now a commonplace that the election of Barack Obama marks the opening of a new period in America's long racial history. The unlikely rise of a black man to the nation's highest office—someone who was a mostly unknown state senator only five years before he was inaugurated president—confirms the view of many, especially whites, that the United States is a postracial society. At last, the shackles of discrimination have been broken and individual merit is rewarded, regardless of skin color. In this view, blackness—once the clearest marker of difference in American society—has lost some or all of its stigma. Barack Obama, in the most common formulation, transcends race; his ancestry fuses African and European into a new hybrid; his political vision of unity discredits those who cling bitterly to notions of racial superiority and, at the same time, rebukes those who harbor a divisive identity politics fueled by an exaggerated sense of racial grievance.

As with all interpretations of the relationship between the past and the present, the notion that Obama's election marks an epochal change in racial dynamics is not without its critics. Obama himself offers a tempered view, suggesting that even if America has advanced considerably over the last forty years, some racial prejudices remain in place and some racial discrimination still exists. In his view, we have realized much, but not all, of the dream of racial equality. Other commentators, like Berkeley historian David Hollinger, suggest that Obama heralds the emergence of a new, multihued racial order, a majority-minority society where static notions of race are losing their purchase, and where race-specific remedies like affirmative action have outlived their usefulness. Many scholars and pundits further to the left, by contrast, are skeptical that much has changed at all. They point to the angry denunciations of Obama during his campaign and since his inauguration (Obama as Muslim, Obama as black man in whiteface, Obama as witch doctor, Obama as noncitizen) as evidence of a deep-seated racism that is inflamed by the discomfiting presence of a brown-hued man in the White House. In the most dystopian vision, offered by Duke sociologist Eduardo Bonilla-Silva, the symbolism of an African-descended president obscures a deeper, more troubling reality: the "Latin Americanization" of the United States, namely, the emergence of a society where a tripartite system of color gradation will supplant the "one-drop rule" of racial classification, but where the darkest-skinned racial minorities remain concentrated at the bottom.[1]

Whether any of these interpretations are right remains to be seen. The past is littered with predictions—usually offered with utter certainty—that proved to be completely wrong. Despite the tragedies of the past century, teleological views of history maintain a powerful grip on our imaginations. But if the moral arc of the universe bends toward justice, it just as often veers off course. Whether optimistic, tempered, or pessimistic, our visions of the present and the uncertain future are shaped by our understandings of the past, for to predict something new means that an old order—a historical phase— seems to be or is passing. When it comes to race and equality, our visions of the past and future depend on how we interpret the most important social and political movement in modern American history: the struggle for civil rights, black power, and racial equality.

By virtue of his life story, the racial identity that he has chosen and the one that he has had chosen for him, his intellect, and his political ambition, Barack Obama has become both America's first African American president and the nation's most influential historian of race and civil rights. About race and its legacy in the United States, Obama has been occasionally candid and but more often coy and indirect, for it quickly became conventional wisdom that "injecting race" into national politics was a risky strategy. Yet for all of its political risks, race is a topic that has animated Obama's entire adult life, from his explorations of black power in college, to his work as a community organizer in Chicago, to his career as a politician representing a mostly black district in the Illinois State Senate. No nationally prominent political figure—at least since Lyndon Johnson and Martin Luther King, Jr.—has offered such detailed reflections on race as Obama's in his two memoirs and in some of his key political speeches, especially in Philadelphia in March 2008, in the aftermath of a firestorm provoked by the release of videotapes of sermons by his pastor, Jeremiah Wright, Jr. Even when Obama has raised racial issues offhandedly, they have become national news. His aside, in August 2008, that he did not resemble other presidents on dollar bills, led his opponent John McCain to accuse him of "playing the race card, and playing it from the bottom of the deck." And his brief commentary on the arrest of Harvard professor Henry Louis Gates, Jr., at the end of a fifty-minute-long press conference on health care in July 2009, led to weeks of heated debate. Obama's mere mention of race in the peculiar political climate of early twenty-first-century America led critics to label him as racist, divisive, and a monger of racial grievances, or, conversely, as courageous, prophetic, and a truth teller.

In *The Audacity of Hope,* his 2005 political memoir, Obama admitted that "I serve as a blank screen on which people of vastly different political stripes project their own views." On race, however, Obama is more than a blank screen. Over the course of his political career he developed a distinctive view of his own place in America's racial history and used that reading of history to mold his political career. After experimenting with different narratives of the history of black power, black politics, and civil rights, Obama fashioned a personal and political identity that rested on a single, powerful, and conventional reading of modern American history. It is one that reinforced a grand narrative of racial reconciliation, an account of America moving inexorably toward racial equality, or, as Obama put it in his most famous speech, "toward a more perfect union." The power of Obama's understanding of race comes from its fundamental optimism, its articulation of a deeply American belief in the inevitability of progress. How Obama understands America's history of race is not simply a matter of biographical interest, for the ways that we recount the history of racial inequality and civil rights—the narratives that we construct about our past—guide our public policy priorities and our lawmaking and, even more fundamentally, shape our national identity. Barack Obama's powerful evocation of the past to fashion a message of hope and reconciliation is more revealing about the racial politics of modern America than it is about the past or about the relationship of that past to our present.

And likewise, Obama, the most intellectual of presidents since Woodrow Wilson, developed a powerful and politically pragmatic analysis of the relationship of racial discrimination, economic restructuring, family dysfunction, and poverty. He fused together his experience as a resident, activist, and politician living and working on Chicago's South Side with a sociological understanding of race, class, and inequality. Obama encountered the deindustrialization, urban disinvestment, and everyday insecurity of Chicago's poor with the eyes of a social scientist, the heart of a churchgoer, and the political pragmatism of a centrist Democrat. Combining these attributes, he built on and reinforced an important shift in understandings of race and the underclass that reoriented both social science and public policy in turn-of-the-century America.

≋

This book is a history of the recent past. It spans the period from the late 1970s to 2009, the adult lifetime of Barack Obama. It is not a conventional biography, but rather three thematic essays that situate Obama squarely in the context of late twentieth- and early twenty-first-century American politics, intellectual life, culture, and society. Obama came to an understanding of race in a particular historical period—in a time of sociological paradox, ideological confusion, and intense debate about racial politics that followed the "classic phase" of the civil rights movement. He came of age as part of a generation of African-descended Americans who found opportunities unimaginable only a few decades earlier, but who also lived in a society when, at the same time, many of the measures of racial inequality worsened. He entered public life at a moment when racial controversies roiled urban neighborhoods and college campuses and dominated partisan politics, including Republican efforts to capture disaffected white Southerners and Democratic efforts to retain the allegiance of disaffected blue-collar whites. Race figured centrally in key debates over late twentieth-century public policies including welfare, affirmative action, criminal justice, and education. Obama's understanding of America's racial past, his interpretation of the social dynamics of race in the present, and his vision of the future all bear the marks of his experience coming of age and entering public life in post-1960s America.

My approach in this book is to bridge intellectual, cultural, political, and social history, exploring Obama as intellectual (someone who has thought broadly about race in American society, and who has engaged, often deeply, with social scientific and religious thought about poverty and inequality); Obama as politician (someone who has crafted a public image, one that includes a rereading of civil rights history, in service of building a winning electoral coalition); and Obama as policymaker (someone who combines intellectual analysis and political calculation in choosing what public policies to support, which to downplay or neglect, and which to oppose).

To understand Obama's life and times requires an examination of race and racial politics. It is safe to say that few domestic issues have been more controversial in late twentieth- and early twenty-first-century America. And few issues have generated more passion among scholars and journalists. Debates about civil rights, black power, race consciousness, and inequality are often couched in predictable and analytically problematic formulations that reflect the moral dualism that still shapes our understandings of race. The first binary —"race versus class"—inflects much scholarship and liberal journalism about race. Either race matters as a dominant force or it is a screen—or a form of false consciousness—that masks far deeper inequalities of class. This is a simplistic formulation that downplays the ways that racial and economic disadvantages are fundamentally intertwined, and fails to address how the American economy generates inequalities that affect people regardless of their background but are still disproportionately borne by people of color. A second binary —with special hold in public discourse—is "racism versus color blindness." This contrasts a pathology and a principle, a flawed reality and an ideal. But it, too, does not stand up to close scrutiny. As legal scholar Richard Thompson Ford has argued, to hurl the invective "racist" loosely is to put too much weight on individual beliefs or values. And conversely, to proclaim color blindness is to overlook the ways that racial inequalities persist and sometimes harden regardless of the good intentions or the benign disposition of any single actor. There are stone-cold racists in America, and there are people who believe that they are wholly free of prejudice. Ultimately, the most enduring racial inequalities in the United States today are not the consequence of conspiracy or intention, or even the unconscious prejudice that neuropsychologists argue exists in the amygdala; rather they stem from the long-term institutional legacies of economic and public policies that have systematically disadvantaged African Americans and, when left unaltered, continue to do so in key realms of American life today.[2] The third binary is "pessimism versus optimism." Either America is still a profoundly racist society, or we have mostly overcome past racial injustices. Any clear-eyed examination of race in modern America must recognize the changes that have transformed the life chances of African Americans in the United States since the mid-twentieth century, and that enabled Barack Obama's remarkable ascent through some of America's most prestigious institutions and ultimately to the White House—most of them the result of grassroots activism, litigation, and public policy innovation. And it must also account for what even a cursory review of census data, opinion surveys, and health, educational, and housing statistics reveals: namely, that racial gaps are deep and persistent in

American life. Those statistics, the way that Obama understands and interprets them, and the ways that Americans in general make sense of them, are at the heart of this book.

≋

Writing recent history presents many pitfalls. Many authors are engaged in political combat, with a personal or political stake in elevating, maintaining, or diminishing the reputation of a national political figure. Those who have dug into the political trenches, fighting for a particular piece of legislation or battling ideological foes, might be tempted to misread a historical argument as a thinly veiled polemic, or to make assumptions about the author's politics and hunt for his biases. This book is not intended as a pro-Obama or anti-Obama tract; it is not an op-ed or a policy paper. Rather it is informed by my interests as a historian and sociologist trying to make sense of the still-significant reality of race in modern America. For the sake of full disclosure, I note that I voted for Barack Obama in 2008, made a modest financial contribution to his campaign, and served as a member of his campaign's urban policy advisory committee. I have also written opinion pieces and given public lectures that express sympathy with some of his policies, skepticism about some, and outright criticism of others. Yet in the pages that follow, I strive for balance.

My purpose here is neither to write a hagiography of Barack Obama nor to defend him against his political enemies. That will surely disappoint some of his most fervent supporters, like a distinguished academic in the audience at the Lawrence Stone Lectures in Princeton, where I presented an earlier version of this book, who objected to part of my argument because, as she stated, she agrees "with everything that Barack Obama has ever said." In the following pages, I sometimes point out inconsistencies in Obama's thinking about race, but not as an attempt to discredit him by keeping a tally sheet of "flip-flops" (for few if any politicians or ordinary citizens are wholly consistent in their beliefs over time). Nor is my task to measure Obama by the yardstick of authenticity that defines many African American public figures (the oft-raised questions "Is Obama too black?" or "Is Obama not black enough?" are unanswerable and uninteresting). And my approach is not that of many presidential scholars, to highlight such attributes as leadership, greatness, or uniqueness (an assessment of such qualities will be the task of another generation of historians and political scientists with quite different interests from mine). Rather than hurling a polemic, drafting a scorecard, or fighting today's political battles, I offer a historical vantage point on the very recent past, favoring analysis over a blow-by-blow account of newspaper headlines, and privileging the long view over flash-in-the-pan controversies and the passions of the moment.

As much as is possible, I attempt to escape from the straitjacket of current political discourse. For example, I emphasize, where appropriate, Obama's political motivations. This risks misinterpretation because of the way that "political" and "politician" have become pejorative terms in modern American life. And the possibility of misinterpretation is compounded by Obama's own rhetoric. A significant component of his appeal during the campaign of 2008 was that he ran (as have many successful national candidates, especially in the post-Watergate era) as an antipolitician, a reformer who distances himself from the equivocation, self-interest, partisanship, and hyperbole that are inevitably part of electioneering and policymaking. But to take that rhetoric at face value, to view Obama as somehow antipolitical, is to overlook the fact that he fashioned a campaign strategy with a seasoned and effective team of media advisers, speechwriters, and handlers. He raised more money than has any other candidate for higher office in American history, and he used it to craft and disseminate an image that many voters found compelling. So when I describe Obama's use of civil rights history (to take an example from the first chapter) as part of his political image making, that should be read as a straightforward description of what men and women running for office do, not as an attempt to besmirch his reputation by branding him a "mere politician." There is nothing inauthentic about finding an identity, developing an intellectual analysis of social problems, and then repackaging them for political purposes.

This book focuses on just one aspect of Obama's career (and, it should be said, not the one that he has prioritized in his presidency) and on one dimension of America in our times (America's long history of racial division and the struggle for racial representation and equality). Race is important, but it cannot begin to explain everything about contemporary American politics and society. There are many other books to be written about Obama—and many that will not, for good reason, put his racial politics in the center. *Not Even Past* is, by necessity, a first draft of what is a larger and still-unfinished history of race, identity, inequality, and power in modern America. But it is also something more—a reflection on history—and how we remember it, use it, and shape it to understand our present and our future.

I

"This Is My Story":

Obama, Civil Rights, and Memory

≋

"Rosa sat so Martin could walk...
Martin walked, so Obama could run...
Obama is running so our children can fly!"

So goes a poem that circulated widely during the last weeks of the 2008 presidential election.[1] This short piece of verse encapsulates the relationship of Barack Obama to collective memories of the civil rights movement. It is a story of debt: Obama owes his success to the past generation of civil rights protesters. It is a story of redemption: Obama's political career realizes their dream that skin color be no longer a bar to ambition. And it is a story of hope and promise: Obama's victory will open up extraordinary opportunities to the next generation. The poem offers an unself-conscious interpretation of history—it is powerful because it provides Obama with a political genealogy in the most important social movement of the twentieth century and offers a teleological view of America on an inexorable path of progress.

It is by now axiomatic that Obama's election as the first African American president of the United States brought the goals of Parks and King to fruition. November 4, 2008, was, in the words of Henry Louis Gates, Jr., "a magical transformative moment . . . the symbolic culmination of the black freedom struggle, the grand achievement of a great collective dream."[2] In the days following the election, Gallup reported that more than two-thirds of Americans viewed Obama's election as "either the most important advance for blacks in the past 100 years, or among the two or three most important such advances."[3] *Time* magazine reinforced the message, arguing in a postelection cover story that King's dream "is being fulfilled sooner than anyone imagined."[4] Many observers went even further, asserting that the Obama election marked the emergence of a postracial era, the end of racial history, or, in the hyperbolic words of one observer, "a seismic event" that sends the history of civil rights "crashing into apparent obsolescence."[5] Obama's election had particular resonance overseas, confounding deeply held perceptions of the United States as incorrigibly racist that dated back to media coverage of the civil rights struggles of the 1950s and 1960s. The day after the election, a prominent French commentator wrote that "a land of discrimination and relegation, the United States has taken a big step toward redemption." What European observers called the "Obama effect" sparked self-reflective discussions about domestic racism and politics in France, Germany, and Italy, an inversion of the commonplace arguments about America's racist exceptionalism. "We also need to change our preconceptions about American prejudice," wrote the editors of the French left-wing daily *Libération*. "It seems like America could teach us a thing or two about democracy."[6]

The January 2009 inaugural celebrations reinforced the popular belief in Obama's election as the fulfillment of decades of struggle. Two civil rights lions—former SNCC (Student Nonviolent Coordinating Committee) activist and Georgia congressman John Lewis and the Reverend Joseph Lowery, a lieutenant of Martin Luther King, Jr.—sat on the dais below the Capitol dome, embodying Obama's lineage in the Southern freedom struggle. It was a moment unimaginable to those who were bloodied and martyred in the civil rights struggles; arrested at lunch counters in Greensboro, Nashville, and Atlanta; beaten by chain-wielding racists as they fled a burning bus outside Anniston, Alabama; brutalized by fire hoses, billy clubs, and police dogs in Birmingham; murdered and entombed in an earthen dam in Philadelphia, Mississippi; and hauled to jail while marching across the Edmund Pettis Bridge in Selma to demand the right to vote.

Barack Obama himself emphasized his place in the unfolding history of civil rights at key moments during his long presidential campaign, most notably in one of the more extraordinary speeches of his career, at Selma, Alabama, on March 4, 2007, before a mostly black audience at an event commemorating the passage of the Voting Rights Act of 1965. Joining Obama were John Lewis; C. T. Vivian, a minister and close aide to the Reverend King; and Artur Davis, a young, black Harvard law graduate and a Democratic rising star who hoped to be the first African American elected to statewide office in Alabama since Reconstruction.

It was one of Obama's most moving speeches, a virtuosic performance, delivered in the sonorous tones of someone who had learned the art of rhetoric from the pulpit of the black church. Obama seemed to be channeling King himself in his cadence, his mix of exhortation and analysis, and his easy use of biblical imagery. The speech culminated in an extended allusion to the book of Exodus. "So I just want to talk a little about Moses and Aaron and Joshua, because we are in the presence today of a lot of Moseses. We're in the presence today of giants whose shoulders we stand on, people who battled, not just on behalf of African Americans but on behalf of all of America; that battled for America's soul, that shed blood. . . . Like Moses, they challenged Pharaoh, the princes, powers who said that some are atop and others are at the bottom, and that's how it's always going to be." He traced his own lineage to their struggle. "It is because they marched that I got the kind of education I got, a law degree, a seat in the Illinois senate and ultimately in the United States senate." Ultimately the story was one of liberation from bondage. "The previous generation, the Moses generation, pointed the way. They took us 90% of the way there. We still got that 10% in order to cross over to the other side." Obama simultaneously paid respect to the elders of the civil rights struggle, situated his career as their legacy, and offered a story of redemption. For those Americans—especially white Americans—who believed that the struggle for racial equality was nearly finished, these words were a balm.

If the struggle was 90 percent complete, what remained to be done? Raising his voice, Obama exhorted the "Joshua Generation" to remember the freedom struggle of the 1960s, to exhibit "the sense of moral clarity and purpose" of those who came before them, and, in a riff familiar to black churchgoers but surprising to most white commentators, called for parental responsibility, criticizing "daddies not acting like daddies" and exhorting a fictional, feckless "Cousin Pookie" to "get off the couch and register some folks and go to the polls." At the core of the speech was his vision of the civil rights struggle as one of individual initiative and self-transformation. "If you want to change the world," Obama solemnly intoned, "the change has to happen with you first and that is something that the greatest and most honorable of generations has taught us." He reinforced the profoundly individualistic understanding of the freedom struggle and its challenge to hearts and minds.[7]

The metaphor of Moses and Joshua, the freedom fighter and the nation builder, offered a powerful framework for Obama's campaign, one that rooted the rootless Hawaiian in the history of the Southern freedom struggle, but with the past as a prologue to a more glorious future. It was Obama's shorthand explanation of the long sweep of black politics from the legislative gains of the mid-1960s to the early twenty-first century. Obama positioned himself as the heir to King and the civil rights movement, but also as part of a vanguard of black politicians who jettisoned a now untimely and divisive sense of racial grievance and embraced mainstream, "middle-class" (what many commentators interpreted as "white") values, rather than appealing to race consciousness. Moses led the Chosen People from the bondage of racial oppression; Joshua would lead them into a multiracial Canaan, where Egyptian and Jew, white and black, pharaohs and prophets would live side by side. Obama signaled the major theme of his campaign: nation building through the restoration of a common national purpose that Americans could achieve by transcending the old divisions of race, ethnicity, religion, and party. And Obama provided a wide range of political commentators with a compelling—but ultimately problematic—framework for discussing the last fifty years of racial politics in the United States, one that emphasizes discontinuity, generational division, and novelty, suggesting that the United States has decisively entered a "post–civil rights era."[8]

The Moses/Joshua metaphor, for all of its power, does not do justice to Obama's relationship to America's long, unfinished struggle for racial equality. The relation between Obama and civil rights history is at once more powerful and more oblique than the conventional narrative would lead us to believe. To understand Obama's place in modern American history requires going beyond King and Parks, Moses and Joshua, to the real Obama and to the relationship of history, memory, biography, and national politics. The history of civil rights in modern America is one of remembering and forgetting, of inclusion and exclusion.

To understand Obama's relationship to America's racial past—and to make sense of how he places himself in it, including what he left in and what he edited out—requires situating him in the context of the contested cultural, intellectual, and political milieu of the period from the 1960s to the present. It is a story of the personal and the political—of how Obama was formed by the shifting racial dynamics of America, and how he interpreted the relationship of past and present as he pursued his vocation as a politician. It is the story of a journey through one of the most contentious periods of America's racial history, through America's post-1960s multicultural turn, into the syncretic black urban politics of the late twentieth century, onto the contested intellectual and cultural terrain of race and "identity politics" in the late 1980s and 1990s, and finally to a moment in the early twenty-first century when America still lived in the shadow of the unfinished civil rights struggles of the previous century while influential journalists, politicians, and scholars hailed the emergence of a postracial order.

≋

Barack Obama was, by his own telling, an unlikely Joshua. Born in Hawaii in 1961, he was both too young and too distant from the heart of the black freedom struggle to have direct memories of it. Hawaii occupied a distinctive place in America's racial history: it was a polyglot, polychromatic part of the far-flung American empire, a place with a troubled history of conquest and unfree labor. By World War II, the island territory had become "the first strange place," where the very mixing of Asians, Americans of European descent, native islanders, and African Americans was so transgressive that the military feared its becoming a seedbed of "mongrelization." It is no surprise that Barack Obama, Sr., a Kenyan national, and Stanley Ann Dunham, a Kansan of European descent, whose courtship and marriage would have been illegal in many states and offensive in most, found Hawaii a propitious place to begin their short-lived interracial relationship in 1959.[9]

Barack Obama recalled that as a child, he was steeped in the "legend" of Hawaii as America's "one true melting pot." That legend had some basis in reality. The only state without a white majority, Hawaii was home to a diverse population of native islanders and Chinese, Japanese, Korean, Filipino, Samoan, Polynesian, and European settlers. No one group was predominant. As an adult, Obama wistfully recalled "the opportunity that Hawaii offered—to experience a variety of cultures in a climate of mutual respect." But diversity had its limits. As part of a minuscule population of African descent on the islands, he stood apart as a racial other. Hawaii was still encumbered by America's rule of hypodescent, namely, that even "one drop" of African blood was enough to stigmatize a person as a racial inferior. As a young man marked as "black" because of his Kenyan father's bloodlines but who was raised by a white mother and grandparents, Obama found himself grappling with the racial categories that America had exported to its island possession.[10]

If Obama was, in part, the product of a hybrid racial culture in Hawaii, he also came of age in the 1970s, at a moment when notions of race, ethnicity, and national identity were in profound flux throughout the United States. It was the beginning of America's age of multiculturalism, when young blacks looked back to a mythical pan-African past, and "white ethnics" began celebrating their origins after generations of being uprooted from their ancestral homes and encouraged to jettison their foreign ways. What had been stigmatized—whether skin color or ethnic heritage—became a source of self-esteem. In one of the most influential journeys of self-discovery in the 1970s, Alex Haley took television viewers in search of his own, mostly fictional African "roots." Haley's lesson—that to know your history was to know your authentic self—reflected an increasingly influential current in mainstream American education and culture in the 1970s.[11]

As a child in a liberal household at the multicultural moment, Obama first learned of America's history of slavery, freedom, civil rights, and black power from his mother, who saw it as her duty to educate her mixed-race son about his country's history. She introduced him to the iconic photographs of the Southern freedom struggle, "mostly the grainy black and white footage that appears every February during black history month," and she regaled him with uplifting stories of prominent African Americans, including Thurgood Marshall and Sidney Poitier. "My mother gave me a positive self-image of being a black person," Obama recalled in a 1995 interview, even if, "to some extent, she romanticized black life."[12]

Obama's early lessons about race and identity were reinforced in the classroom. Social studies curricula, especially at self-consciously progressive schools like Honolulu's Punahou Academy, which he attended from fifth to twelfth grade, celebrated racial and ethnic diversity, even though more than 90 percent of Obama's graduating class was white. In a photograph that captured the school's self-conscious multiculturalism, Obama appeared with his classmates under a sign reading "mixed races of America." The emphasis on diverse identities at Punahou was a far cry from the typical mid-twentieth-century elementary and high school curricula, which depicted America as fundamentally an Anglo-Saxon, Protestant nation that had absorbed and assimilated other European cultures, while proffering clichéd views of black slaves as happy Sambos, Reconstruction as a period of black misrule, and Native Americans and Pacific Islanders as uncivilized. By Obama's school days, history and social studies textbooks had begun to highlight the nation's history of racial oppression, to depict the United States as a nation of many nations, rather than as a melting pot, and to celebrate the contributions of non-Europeans to American culture, even if curricula still mostly offered scanty coverage of Latinos, Asians, and new immigrants.[13]

As a high school student, Barack Obama embarked on his own quest for authenticity. His classmates recall that he sometimes described himself as hapa—a mixed race Hawaiian —and that he often ate lunch in the "Ethnic Corner," a part of Punahou's cafeteria that mixed-race students made their own. Even if he was still uncertain and uncomfortable about his own African roots, he did not embrace his European-American heritage. Instead, he gravitated toward blackness, growing his hair into an Afro, emulating black basketball stars, and seeking out the company of self-identified black Hawaiians. His search for self-understanding drew him inexorably toward the continental United States, to African America: to Harlem, to the souls of black folks, and to the civil rights and black power movements that played out a world away from his childhood homes.[14]

Obama's adolescent search for his own roots led him first to the canonical works of black writers Richard Wright, James Baldwin, W.E.B. Du Bois, and Langston Hughes. But their accounts of black life did not speak to Obama's already irrepressible optimism or to his experience in Hawaii. "In every page of every book," Obama wrote in his 1995 memoir, *Dreams from My Father*, "in Bigger Thomas and invisible men, I kept finding the same anguish, the same doubt; a self-contempt that neither irony nor intellect seemed able to deflect." He found them "exhausted, bitter men, the devil at their heels." But Obama had an epiphany when he read *The Autobiography of Malcolm X*, written with Alex Haley. As Obama recalled, Malcolm's "repeated acts of self-creation spoke to me." It was telling that a young man who had spent his childhood inhabiting an in-between world of race and ethnicity found himself alienated from those writers who themselves struggled with what Du Bois memorably called their "twoness—an American, a Negro; two souls, two thoughts, two unreconciled strivings; two warring ideals in one dark body, whose dogged strength alone keeps it from being torn asunder." Instead, Obama gravitated toward a mixed-race man—who was nicknamed Detroit Red because of skin and hair color—who rejected his white roots, banished the thought of twoness, and had become an icon of assertive black masculinity and racial pride.[15]

Obama's dalliance with Malcolm sparked his interest in black radicalism. In high school in the late 1970s, he befriended Frank Marshall Davis, a longtime black radical, who had followed a common trajectory from the interracial leftism of the postwar years to a more militant race-conscious politics. A poet, journalist, and sometime labor organizer, Davis had an unkempt, graying Afro hairstyle, his own expression of blackness. Obama was something of a Marshall protégé: the two spent hours together drinking and discussing black life and politics. In one memorable conversation, Davis told Obama that "black people have a reason to hate. That's just the way it is." Davis's sentiments put him in the company of those black militants who eschewed nonviolence and attempted to channel black pride and racial anger into oppositional politics. But there was not much of a black power movement left by the time that Obama was in high school, and even less of one when he attended college (from 1979 to 1983). Black power had never been as powerful or popular as its adherents and the news media had asserted, and by the late 1970s, many of its most vocal proponents had burned out, hardened by sectarian struggle and embittered by police harassment. Many of its most restless practitioners had taken political odysseys far from their 1960s nationalism or Marxism. Black Panther Bobby Seale became a motivational speaker and, later, a cookbook author; CORE's fiery Roy Innis and Floyd McKissick had become Republicans. Others left the public limelight, languishing in jail, living overseas in exile, or retreating into private life. Outside of prisons and scattered college campuses, black radical groups were in tatters.[16]

Even if black power was institutionally weak, it lived on in a mix of racial pride and grievance and a celebration of resistance and African culture, exemplified in the late-night rap sessions that Obama joined with fellow black students at Occidental College in California from 1979 to 1981 and, even more, on the streets and in the shops of Harlem, which he got to know intimately over the next three and a half years as a student at Columbia and a resident of New York City. He spent long days "walking from one end of Manhattan to the other," visiting Harlem's Abyssinian Baptist Church and shooting hoops at neighborhood basketball courts. New York in the early 1980s was America's most heterogeneous city, a place marked by its own peculiar history of racial resentments, home to the country's largest concentration of black nationalists, querulous and splintered over arcane sectarian debates from the late 1960s, finding common cause only in their belief in the irreducible racism of white America and their outrage against police repression.

The pull of Malcolm X and a fascination with black separatism and race consciousness led Obama to New York's pan-African festivals, to Harlem's famous "Speakers' Corner" on 125th Street, to black nationalist bookstores, and, most memorably, to a campus lecture by Black Panther founder Kwame Ture (Stokely Carmichael). Ture's performance left Obama unsettled, especially when the speaker upbraided a well-meaning audience member for her "bourgeois attitudes." But even if Obama never really embraced black radicalism, he remained, at least for a time, sympathetic to it.[17]

≡

If Obama flirted with black nationalism, his time as a community organizer in Chicago, to which I will turn in chapter 2, introduced him to another current of the long black freedom struggle, one that was every bit as militant as black nationalism and built on a black community consciousness, even as its practitioners eschewed the goal of racial separatism. "What really inspired me," Obama recalled in an 2007 interview about his early career, "was the civil rights movement. And if you asked me who my role model was at that time, it would probably be Bob Moses, the famous SNCC [Student Nonviolent Coordinating Committee] organizer. . . . Those were the folks I was really inspired by—the John Lewises, the Bob Moseses, the Fannie Lou Hamers, the Ella Bakers." Obama's choice of these activists—along with his use of the past tense—offers a revealing glimpse into his racial politics and how they shifted over time.[18]

The four were among the most militant in the nonviolent freedom movement—none of them were consensus builders. Lewis memorably bucked the organizers of the 1963 March on Washington by drafting a speech that was scathingly critical of the Kennedy administration's gradualism on civil rights, even if, under pressure, he agreed to excise some of its most inflammatory rhetoric. By 1964, when Lewis traveled North, he joined increasingly militant street protests, like one in Rochdale Village in Queens, New York, where he pointedly argued that "the Negro must revolt against not only the white power structure but also against the Negro leadership that would slow the Negro march to a slow shuffle." For her part, Hamer resisted the entreaties of liberal lions like Hubert Humphrey, Joseph Rauh, and Walter Reuther to soften her demands for the seating of the full delegation of the Mississippi Freedom Democratic Party at the 1964 Democratic National Convention. Much to the chagrin of party leaders—including President Lyndon Johnson—she refused to sacrifice racial justice for party unity.[19]

Baker and Moses, in particular, provided interesting analogies for Obama. Both launched their careers in the North. Baker was a left-leaning activist in Harlem in the 1930s, swept into the Popular Front alliance of civil rights activists and Communists. Moses, a native New Yorker and schoolteacher, led SNCC's mostly off-camera organizing in the Mississippi Delta. Both—like Obama, working on Chicago's South Side—viewed community organizing as a discipline, not simply as a tactic (even if they came from different, but related, organizing traditions). Both Baker and Moses were among the most revered activists of their generation—but unlike Obama, who quickly learned the power of his own personal narrative and wove it into his speeches, his writing, and his interviews—both were intensely private, preferring to remain in the background, doing the hard, everyday work of organizing, but seldom serving as spokespeople for the movement and leaving their personal lives hidden from even their closest associates. Obama was an activist-politician whose sensibilities and style emerged in the confessional culture of the post-1960s era; Baker and Moses, by contrast, exhibited a reticence born of the notion that, ultimately, their personal stories did not matter.[20]

In the 1960s, Moses, Baker, Hamer, and Lewis had combined elements of the prophetic and the disruptive in their work. Each was committed to the power of the ballot box, but only Lewis and Hamer aspired to political office. Grassroots organizing and protest did not provide skills that translated easily into the art of electoral politics and lawmaking. Hamer ran two quixotic campaigns for Congress but faced insuperable obstacles to her election in the barely post–Voting Rights Act South. And, by the late 1960s, she had joined the welfare rights movement, advocating for the expansion of citizenship rights for impoverished women—and calling for a destigmatization of welfare. She was ultimately more prophet than politician. Neither Moses nor Baker, like most grassroots activists, aspired to electoral politics. They preferred remaining behind the scenes. Lewis, by contrast, ultimately ran a successful campaign for Congress from an overwhelmingly black congressional district in Georgia, although he used his position less to legislate than to serve as a voice of conscience and a national advocate for racial equality.

≡

As a voracious reader of civil rights and black history, and as a keen observer of black social movements, Obama arrived at a sophisticated understanding of the syncretism that defined black politics. In an essay that he wrote in 1988, Obama argued that "[f]rom W.E.B. Du Bois to Booker T. Washington to Marcus Garvey to Malcolm X to Martin Luther King, this internal debate has raged between integration and nationalism, between accommodation and militancy, between sit-down strikes and boardroom negotiations. The lines between these strategies have never been simply drawn, and the most successful black leadership has recognized the need to bridge these seemingly divergent approaches." Obama perceived the fundamental pragmatism that animated the long black freedom struggle: few activists were ideologically pure. They debated, revised, and reformulated their political positions, rejecting strategies that did not seem to be working, experimenting with new ones, and forging alliances that, to many outside observers who expected ideological consistency, seemed unlikely. Civil rights and black power were fundamentally intertwined in ways that most commentators—trapped in a binaristic framework that pitted the two against each other as irreconcilable—could not grasp.[21]

Obama's description of the synergies between integration and nationalism, between Malcolm and Martin, was an apt description of black politics in the post-1960s years. Over Obama's lifetime, the color of American politics had changed dramatically. In 1965, only 193 blacks held elected office nationwide; just twenty years later, the year that Obama began working as a community activist and political organizer in Chicago, that figure had risen to 6,016. But black politics defied simple characterization. That was a reality that Obama discovered when he moved to the Windy City in the summer of 1985. The city's racial politics were in flux, in large part because of the rise of Harold Washington, elected the city's first black mayor in 1983.

Like so many black politicians, Washington was neither Moses nor Joshua, neither an integrationist nor a race-conscious militant, but rather both. Black electoral politics in the four decades between the passage of the Voting Rights Act and the beginning of Obama's presidential campaign was anything but monolithic. Some politicians were the heirs of black power, particularly those with safe seats in overwhelmingly black districts, who did not depend on white electoral support and who could use explicit race-based appeals to rouse their supporters. They had incentives to adopt a politics of race pride and consciousness. In the handful of majority-black cities (notably Newark, Gary, Washington, and Detroit), black candidates often donned dashikis, engaged in theatrical denunciations of whites, and described their candidacies in terms of black power (even though many real black power advocates lacked the patience, the political skills, and the willingness to be "co-opted" by the two mainstream political parties necessary to win elected office, and conversely many ostensible militants made their peace with white business leaders and civic elites). Detroit mayor Coleman A. Young, who served for twenty years, fired up his black constituents by denouncing suburban whites and arguing that he was "a black first and a Democrat second." Newark's Sharpe James accused his black critics of being racial sellouts and Uncle Toms. And Washington, D.C.'s Marion Berry revived his political career by declaring the scandals that unraveled his mayoralty to have been the result of a white conspiracy. In racially divided cities, congressional, state legislative, and city councilmanic districts were often segregated—and there, too, candidates for political office (both black and white) often found it advantageous to stoke their constituents' fears or appeal to their sense of turf. For a time, especially in the 1970s, campaign posters in majority-black districts appeared not in red, white, and blue, but instead in the red, green, and black of the pan-African flag.[22]

But black militancy was only one thread of post-1960s black politics, even if, because of their rhetoric, its proponents dominated the airwaves. From the 1960s onward, many of the most influential and effective black politicians were—by disposition and necessity—coalition builders. Mostly forgotten in political accounts of the civil rights era was Edward Brooke, a black Massachusetts Republican, who won election to the U.S. Senate in 1966, at a moment of extraordinary racial tension in a 97 percent white state. That summer, Stokely Carmichael uttered the famous words "black power"; welfare rights activists demonstrated at the State House; and antibusing activists Pixie Palladino and Louise Day Hicks won widespread support in Boston's Irish and Italian neighborhoods. Yet Brooke distanced himself from Massachusetts's racially polarized politics: most notably, he distanced himself from Carmichael and persuaded suburban and small-town whites that he was a good-government, fiscally responsible candidate. As a result, he won by a comfortable margin, picking up many Democratic voters, even if he lost big among Boston's bitter blue-collar whites, whose votes he did not need because of the breadth of his coalition. As a Republican, Brooke was an outlier among black politicians, but many of them shared his challenge: how to win office in majority-white jurisdictions.[23]

In the three decades after Brooke's election, sixty-seven cities with populations over fifty thousand elected black mayors, nearly all of them members of the Democratic Party. Most of those cities were majority white. Many black leaders—even those with origins in the controversial community control and black power movements of the 1960s—forged political coalitions across racial lines, although an admixture of racism and antiliberalism kept most of them from winning a white majority. In 1973, Tom Bradley won election as mayor of Los Angeles, a city with a relatively small black population (only 17.7 percent of the city's inhabitants), still struggling with the divisive legacy of the 1965 Watts riot. In 1983, Wilson Goode, who had started his career as a community organizer with funds from the War on Poverty, was elected mayor of

Philadelphia, a majority-white city, with the support of almost a quarter of white voters. Blacks won elected office, with white support, in many other majority-white cities, among them Baltimore, New Haven, and Denver.[24]

Black electoral gains (outside of the majority-minority districts created after the Voting Right Act of 1965) were slower to come in the South, but there, too, black politicians who aspired to statewide office forged successful interracial electoral coalitions. In 1983, voters in Charlotte, North Carolina, a majority-white city and bastion of the New New South, a place with its own deep divisions over civil rights and school desegregation, put moderate black businessman Harvey Gantt into office. In an intensely polarized race for the U.S. Senate in 1990, Gantt barely lost to incumbent Republican Jesse Helms, who rallied his supporters by playing to fears of racial quotas and white job loss. Virginia, once capital of the Confederacy, elected a black Democratic governor, Douglas Wilder, in 1989. Both of these candidates shifted to the right of their black constituents, positioning themselves as pro-business and socially moderate, assuming correctly that they would lose little black support, while gaining white support. One crossed the racial divide, and the other nearly did, both in states with long histories of racial animosity.[25]

On the national level, too, the gap between Moses and Joshua was blurry. African American women, many of them coalition builders, played a decisive role in reconfiguring liberal politics. Shirley Chisholm, elected to Congress from Brooklyn in 1968, became the first African American Democratic candidate for president. In 1976, Texas congresswoman Barbara Jordan delivered a celebrated keynote address nominating Jimmy Carter (whose centrist presidential candidacy, it should be noted, was ardently supported by such alleged race-baiters as Coleman Young). Chisholm and Jordan did not get very far nationally, not because they were politicians steeped in the race-conscious identity politics of the civil rights years, but rather because the majority of white voters were unwilling to cross the racial divide.

The multiple currents that shaped black urban politics coursed through twentieth-century Chicago. The Windy City had a long history of black-white collaboration—and co-optation—through the city's powerful Democratic machine. From the 1920s onward, many aspiring black politicians made their peace with the city's machine, in exchange for patronage jobs, walking-around money, and a modicum of power. With machine support—and at the cost of their political independence—Oscar de Priest, Arthur Mitchell, and William L. Dawson served as the twentieth century's first three black U.S. representatives. As the city's black population grew during the World War II era, the city's white leadership paid more heed to their black constituents, even if they were parsimonious, saving the best municipal positions for whites. By the 1960s, a growing number of civil rights and black power activists rebelled against the machine, creating a small but spirited independent movement. The machine's hold on black voters weakened in the 1960s and 1970s, as the city's blacks were alienated by the anti–civil rights and no-holds-barred law-and-order policies of the Daley administration. In the 1970s and 1980s, former civil rights and black power activists began to run for political office and win, among them Obama's Democratic rival in his first state senate race, Alice Palmer; and his opponent in his failed 2000 bid for Congress, former Black Panther Bobby Rush.[26]

No one better embodied the syncretic nature of black electoral politics than did Harold Washington, a candidate who came up through the Chicago machine but then broke from it to run as a reform candidate. Washington fashioned a dual

strategy for victory: he appealed to the racial pride and grievances of his black constituents, while reaching out to an interracial constituency. He came to office amid a black urban
backlash against the Reagan administration, whose economic
policies had worsened inner-city economies, whose "New
Federalism" led to a steady reduction in urban spending, and
whose challenges to affirmative action and welfare reinforced
racial stereotypes. Washington swept to victory in large part
because of the huge turnout among his African American
base—after a massive voter registration campaign, 70 percent
of Chicago's eligible black voters cast their ballots.[27]

The political potency of black consciousness left a deep im-
pression on Obama. He observed that Chicago's blacks talked
about the mayor "with a familiarity and affection normally
reserved for a relative." It was Harold, not Mayor Washington (just as it had been Martin, Malcolm, Huey, and Jesse—
and, twenty years later, in barbershops, churches, and the
black blogosphere, it would be Barack). After Washington's
victory, Chicago's blacks had taken to the streets by the thousands in celebration, a massive expression of racial pride and
triumph over the city's long-dominant white power structure.
As Obama walked through the South Side in the mid-1980s,
he could not help but notice the icons of Harold. "His picture
was everywhere: on the walls of shoe repair shops and beauty
parlors, still glued to the lampposts from the last campaign...
like some protective totem."[28]

Black loyalty to Washington was, in part, a matter of group
pride, but also a matter of self-interest. Political power brought
real economic benefits to urban blacks. By the 1960s, the public sector had become an important avenue of upward mobility for black workers, even if they had mostly been confined
to unskilled, bottom-of-the-rung jobs like sanitation work. In
many cities, including Chicago, municipal jobs were unionized

and secure, with generous health and pension benefits, and they provided a compelling alternative to rapidly disappearing manufacturing work. But black workers were not satisfied with entry-level, manual labor. Empowered by the civil rights movement—and its call for jobs, dignity, and freedom—they demanded inclusion in better-paying, mostly white firefighting, police, teaching, and clerical jobs. And black businesses demanded access to lucrative city contracts. Washington's election brought real gains. Like other black mayors, he hired more black workers, expanded affirmative action programs, and extended more contracts to minority-owned firms, in the process undoing years of machine neglect.[29]

But Washington was not just the "black candidate" or the "black mayor," even if, in racially polarized Chicago, black voters overwhelmingly supported him and the vast majority of white voters opposed his candidacy vehemently. Eighty-one percent of Chicago's whites—who were preponderantly Democrats—broke party ranks and supported Republican Bernard Epton, bringing him within thousands of votes of victory in 1983. But Washington drew support from Chicago's rapidly growing Latino population and from white liberals who provided him with campaign funds and enough votes to put him over the top. As mayor, Washington rewarded his supporters, especially African Americans, with positions in his administration, even though Chicago's infamous "council wars," led by powerful, race-baiting alderman "Fast Eddie" Vrydolyak, held up many mayoral appointments. But at the same time he surrounded himself with an interracial team of advisers, including two figures who would later be members of Obama's inner circle: David Axelrod (a Jewish-American former journalist who went on to a career managing the campaigns of many black mayors, including Detroit's Dennis Archer, Cleveland's Michael White, and Philadelphia's John

Street) and Valerie Jarrett (an African American lawyer who became a major player in post-Washington Chicago politics and real estate). Washington also made peace with leading white politicians (endorsing Richard M. Daley, his onetime opponent and son of the longtime machine leader, and Aurelia Pucinski, daughter of powerful congressman and white ethnic spokesman Roman Pucinski, in their bids for Cook County offices). And Washington worked to overcome the suspicion of Chicago's business elite by cutting the city's payroll, reducing the city's debt, and restoring its favorable credit rating. As a consequence, Chicago's black nationalists—many of whom had enthusiastically supported his candidacy—charged him with "accommodationism." Washington's ability to build coalitions, while simultaneously appealing to his black base, was the key to his victory, just as it would be for Obama a quarter century later.[30]

Washington's rise to power coincided with the political reinvention of another Chicagoan who would move on to the national stage, the Reverend Jesse L. Jackson, Sr. An aide to Martin Luther King, Jr., Jackson had followed a circuitous course through black politics that also defied easy characterization. An advocate of economic integration as the head of the Southern Christian Leadership Conference's Operation Breadbasket in the mid-1960s, he shifted toward black power after King's assassination and, by the early 1970s, advocated the creation of a black-only political party. Jackson also flirted with the Republicans on and off through 1980, in part because of his distrust of Chicago's white Democratic Party regulars, in part because of his staunch opposition then to legalized abortion. But Washington's successful efforts to build a coalition of minorities and liberal whites suggested another path for Jackson. In the 1980s, Jackson jettisoned his social conservatism and fashioned a politics that emphasized the interconnections between economic and racial justice—returning to a theme that had animated King's career.[31]

Jackson's critics lambasted him for political opportunism, for his singular and some would say inflated sense of his importance as a civil rights leader, and for his ideological inconsistency, but even with those liabilities he made a signature contribution to Democratic Party politics in the mid-1980s. Rather than accepting racial polarization as a given, Jackson advocated interracial coalition building, accepting the diversity of the party but calling for a class politics that would allow blacks, whites, and Latinos to ally on the basis of their shared economic interests. He named it the "rainbow coalition." Much to the surprise of political commentators, in 1988 Jackson won Democratic primaries and caucuses in eleven states, including Michigan, ground zero of the Reagan Democrats, by appealing to Detroit's blacks and to working-class white voters who were victims of the state's troubled economy. And although his campaign struggled with gaffes—most notably his anti-Semitic jibe that New York was "Hymie-Town"—he continued to push for a politics that transcended race. In his speech at the 1988 Democratic national convention, one of the most memorable in recent history, Jackson sounded themes of racial reconciliation that would reverberate in Obama's campaign two decades later. Although Jackson's streetwise style, his sometimes overwrought, preacherly rhetoric, and his history hindered his aspiration to higher office, the substance of his message—his celebration of America as a "patchwork quilt," diverse yet united—was remarkably similar to Obama's. Even if he offered too simple a political genealogy, Alton Miller, who served as Washington's press secretary, was not wrong when he observed that "[w]hat Harold did helped make Jesse more credible, and what Jesse did helped make Barack more credible, and so it goes."[32]

For all of his affinities to Washington and Jackson, Obama expressed ambivalence about Chicago's two most visible black politicians. Writing shortly after Washington's untimely death (he passed away in 1987, just months into his second term in office), Obama wrote that "Harold Washington and Jesse Jackson are but two striking examples of how the energy and passion of the Civil Rights movement have been channeled into bids for more traditional political power." Obama hailed Washington's willingness to stand up to Chicago's machine leaders. But rather than understanding Washington as a coalition builder, he portrayed him as the embodiment of race-conscious politics, noting "the surge of political empowerment around the country" that had fired up black voters. But for Obama, the "only principle that came through" during Washington's administration was "getting our fair share,'" namely, efforts to use the power of the mayoralty for black group advancement, and that did not suffice. Obama was skeptical that black political power, like Washington's mayoralty, would have anything more than "an important symbolic effect." What Obama left out was perhaps the most important part of Washington's relatively progressive policy: his efforts to channel community development block grants to neighborhood groups, to shift development dollars toward the construction of affordable housing, and to increase capital spending to improve the city's poor and working-class neighborhoods. Each of these initiatives met with significant resistance, both from those developers and planners who favored large-scale downtown redevelopment and from Washington's aldermanic opponents. Overall, Obama echoed those political analysts who viewed the black ascent to urban power as a "hollow prize," the dubious triumph of taking over local governments just as jobs were disappearing, population steadily declining, and tax revenue plummeting. City jobs for black Chicagoans were not enough to stem the effects of decades of disinvestment. Pinstripe patronage for black entrepreneurs would not benefit the poor. And the problems facing urban residents were larger than any single elected official could solve.[33]

≋

When Obama left Chicago for Harvard Law School in 1988, he soon found himself in the center of a racial battleground every bit as acrimonious as Harold Washington's Chicago, even if the stakes were not nearly as high. Obama was an outsider during Chicago's council wars, but he was deeply involved in the "culture wars" of the late 1980s and the early 1990s—skirmishes over race, identity, and politics that played out with special intensity among public intellectuals and on campuses. A formative experience in Obama's intellectual development, the culture wars fundamentally reoriented his interpretation of racial politics. By the early 1990s, Obama began to distance himself from what he saw as the polarizing politics of civil rights and race, toward a position that emphasized racial reconciliation.

If the distinctions between civil rights and black power—between Malcolm and Martin—were always blurry in practice, by the mid-1980s journalists and academics drew bright lines between them, and often polemically, as a Manichaean struggle between a civic universalism on one hand and a narrow particularism on the other. A growing cadre of white liberals called for a restoration of the New Deal order, longing for a past when a shared class consciousness had supplanted a divisive ethnoracial politics. And others called for a resuscitation of a common American creed of equality and opportunity, and a rejection of race consciousness and multiculturalism. Writing in the age of Reagan, they lamented the waning of social democracy—but they turned inward, blaming race-conscious leftists even more than conservatives for the "unraveling" of liberalism. In the late 1980s, their sense of crisis was heightened by highly publicized racial conflicts, especially in New York. They focused their attention on racially divisive street protests led by angry rhetoricians, usually men without large organizational bases but with considerable talent, most prominently the Reverend Al Sharpton (who had burst onto the national scene in late 1987 as the defender of Tawana Brawley, an African American teenager whose fabricated story of a violent rape and cover-up conspiracy dominated headlines). Equally culpable for racial polarization were controversial black mayors like Coleman Young and Sharpe James. The mainstream media's fascination with those "race men" overshadowed the more numerous, usually quieter, and more influential community activists, clerics, and political leaders, many of them women (the forgotten Miriams of the black freedom struggle), who often did not play to the cameras. Influential journalists mostly overlooked the legion of black politicians who forged interracial coalitions and often collaborated closely with white political and business leaders.[34]

At the same time, an influential group of academics and journalists turned their often formidable talents to retelling the history of civil rights, especially in the North, usually from the vantage point of aggrieved working- and middle-class whites. Accounts of the Boston busing crisis and racial strife in Brooklyn—two of the bloodiest battlegrounds in the Northern freedom struggle—offered sympathetic portrayals of urban ethnics who viewed affirmative action as a zero-sum game, resented school desegregation as the meddling of "limousine liberals," and were bitter at civil rights leaders' representations of their politics as incorrigibly racist. In these narratives, white working-class and lower-middle-class Northerners, a minority of whom ever supported the black freedom struggle, even at its peak in the mid-1960s, were recast as well-meaning, incipient racial liberals who would have joined an interracial coalition had they not been alienated by the "excesses" of the civil rights movement and black power.[35]

Parallel controversies about race and identity roiled universities—including Obama's Harvard—in the late 1980s and early 1990s. A vocal, interracial group of leftists, mostly based in humanities departments and law schools, embraced the politics of diversity and difference. Their opponents, a mix of embattled campus conservatives, disaffected liberals, and public intellectuals, rose up to defend the university against them. The most heated battles in the campus culture wars were fought over race and representation: namely, the merits of affirmative action in higher education and the inclusion of minorities and women in the curriculum. Should difference and race consciousness be cultivated in the classroom, or should the mission of higher education be color-blind and universalistic? Those on the right branded advocates of difference as "politically correct," and those on the left argued that their opponents marginalized the voices of the oppressed.[36]

When Barack Obama arrived at Harvard Law School in the fall of 1988, he found himself on the Eastern Front of the culture wars. Harvard was racked with controversies over racial politics in the classroom and the racial composition of the faculty. In spring 1988, the semester before Obama arrived at Harvard, the campus bitterly divided over accusations that history professor Stephan Thernstrom was racially insensitive. Students in a course that he taught on race and ethnicity accused him of silencing the voices of blacks by assigning pro-slavery tracts but not slave narratives, and they charged him with using his lectures to promote conservative views on affirmative action, the black family, and urban poverty. Thernstrom countered that his critics practiced latter-day "McCarthyism," silencing their academic adversaries and imposing a stifling leftist ideological conformity in the classroom.[37]

Harvard Law School in the late 1980s was an especially contentious place, so much so that it was nicknamed the "Beirut of legal education." During Obama's second year at Harvard (1989–90), the law school exploded in racial controversy. When the HLS faculty did not make a job offer to visiting faculty member Regina Austin, an African American professor from the University of Pennsylvania, the Black Law Students Association (of which Obama was a member) accused the law school dean of racism, railed against the fact that Harvard had no tenured black women and only a handful of nonwhite faculty members, and led a series of teach-ins and protests, including a sit-in at the dean's office, to demand the diversification of the law school. Derrick Bell, the law school's first tenured black faculty member, took a "leave of conscience" in protest (and later resigned his post). Members of Harvard's chapter of the Federalist Society, a conservative legal group, criticized affirmative action and contended that any policies to mandate diversity in Harvard's student body and faculty would sacrifice quality by undermining the principle of meritocracy. Both sides wrapped themselves in the mantle of the civil rights movement. The black students claimed that their protest was in the tradition of the black freedom struggle—indeed at one rally, Obama compared Bell to Rosa Parks. And conservative students countered that they were being faithful to Martin Luther King, Jr.'s vision of a color-blind society, and that Austin's supporters were practitioners of a divisive identity politics rooted in black power.[38]

Despite his sympathies with Austin and Bell, Obama positioned himself as someone who could reconcile Harvard's bitter differences by bringing a tone of civility to the debate. He refused to denounce his critics and hurl polemics. In the words of Bradford Berenson, a conservative student who would later work in the second Bush administration, "Even though he was clearly a liberal, he didn't appear to the conservatives in the review to be taking sides in the tribal warfare." Obama's position in the middle allowed him to build a winning coalition of liberals and conservatives in his bid to be elected president of the *Harvard Law Review* in February 1990. Later that year, in a dispute about the law review's affirmative action policy, Obama again attempted to reconcile the opposing camps. He defended the principle of affirmative action while suggesting that he respected the "depth and sincerity" of its opponents' beliefs. Racial preferences, he contended, would "enhance the representativeness" of the law review's staff, but not "at the price of any 'lower standard' of editorial excellence." Obama's intervention did not lead to anything more than a momentary cease-fire in Harvard's culture wars. The law school continued to be intensely polarized. Still, it was a defining moment in his racial education.[39]

Obama's experience at Harvard tempered his sympathy for the race-conscious politics of the black freedom struggle. His emphasis on reconciliation over confrontation dovetailed with his ongoing search for an identity—a defining story, a way to make sense of American history and his place in it. That journey inevitably led him back in time to the Jim Crow South—a place whose indignities and struggles he had not experienced, except through his mother's stories. Obama eventually found himself drawn to "a series of images, romantic images of a past I had never known." His search for authenticity and purpose led him to "the sit-ins, the marches, the jailhouse songs" of the Southern struggle for civil rights.[40] There, on the streets of Birmingham, in the pews of Atlanta, in the jails of Mississippi, Obama found himself, his community, and his calling. "This is my story," Obama excitedly told a friend in the late 1980s, after reading Taylor Branch's *Parting the Waters*, the Pulitzer Prize–winning first volume of his epic biography of Martin Luther King, Jr. How Barack Obama read and used that history shaped both his political agenda and his political persona.[41]

≋

When Obama returned to Chicago in 1991, his view of civil rights and black politics was still in flux. The lessons that he had learned about black empowerment from observing Harold Washington's career shaped his first post–law school political venture. In 1992, he coordinated a citywide voter registration campaign that proved to be crucial for the election of Carol Moseley Braun as the first black woman and only the second African American senator since Reconstruction: more than 100,000 minority voters were registered. Like many successful black politicians in the post-1960s years, Braun fashioned a dual campaign, appealing to liberal white voters in Chicago's suburbs and downstate (especially well-educated women), while also mobilizing African American voters. Coalition building and race-conscious political mobilization once again went hand in hand. Obama, who had studied voting rights law at Harvard, also took a position that was unpopular among many conservative critics of civil rights: he argued, both in the classroom and in the public arena, for the creation and maintenance of majority-minority jurisdictions, as a tool for black political advancement. "As long as we have hardened racial attitudes reflected in our voting patterns for minorities," stated Obama, "to elect one of their own, they still need to have a substantial voting-age majority in neighborhoods and communities." Obama argued that "we need to ensure that minorities have a voice in all corridors of power."[42]

But for Obama, race-conscious political mobilization was not a hard-and-fast ideological position; it was a pragmatic one. By the mid-1990s, that pragmatism shaped his emerging critique of race-conscious politics. "Nationalism," he wrote in his memoir, *Dreams from My Father*, "dissipated into an attitude rather than any concrete program, a collection of grievances and not an organized force, images and sounds that crowded the airwaves but without any corporeal existence." At its worst, black militancy pandered to the media, for "like sex or violence on TV, black rage always found a ready market." The ultimate flaw of black radicalism, in Obama's view, was that it was performative, not practical. "It was like a bad dream," he recalled. "The movement had died years ago, shattered into a thousand fragments. Every path to change was well-trodden, every strategy exhausted."[43]

Eager for his own concrete program, Obama launched his campaign for the Illinois State Senate in 1995. It was in post-Washington Chicago that Obama learned how to play hardball politics. Sympathetic to Washington's reform impulse and in the tradition of politicians who represented the fiercely independent Hyde Park neighborhood (Obama's home and political base), he kept Chicago's machine at arm's length. But even as he rhetorically distanced himself from the messiness of Chicago-style politics, he learned to play rough quickly; his tactics included removing his state senate opponent, Alice Palmer, a civil rights activist turned legislator, from the ballot in his first run for office in 1996, arousing the ire of some prominent South Side leaders.[44]

In his eight years as Illinois state senator representing liberal Hyde Park and the adjoining, predominantly black South

Side, Obama focused on issues mostly of concern to his minority constituents. He pushed for legislation to address racial profiling (even suggesting that he had been pulled over for "driving while black"); championed urban job creation programs, an especially important issue in the job-poor South Side; argued for an expansion of the earned income tax credit (EITC); backed legislation to remediate lead paint (a major health hazard, especially for children living in old, rundown housing); and advocated more generous state support for inner-city schools. Representing a racially mixed and socioeconomically diverse district honed Obama's instincts on coalition building. To reach his well-educated constituents in the area around the University of Chicago, he wrote a regular column for the *Hyde Park Herald*, a neighborhood newspaper of unusually high quality. He held living room fund-raisers that attracted a mix of Hyde Park residents: professors, nonprofit executives, and other professionals. He stumped in black churches and met frequently with black civic groups.[45]

But Obama's coalition-building skills did not always serve his political career. Many local black political leaders considered him arrogant, more closely connected to his university neighborhood than to the surrounding communities. When he challenged popular Bobby Rush, a former Black Panther and city alderman, who had won election to the U.S. House of Representatives in 1992, Obama faced a humiliating defeat. Rush was one of a rare breed of former black power activists with the political skills to get elected to higher office. His history served him well in the working-class neighborhoods of the South Side. As a politician who represented a racially homogeneous district, Rush did not have to cultivate voters across racial lines, allowing him to play to his constituents' racial pride without political risk. Even though Obama lost by a two-to-one margin, he used his campaign to strengthen his political connections among Chicago's white power brokers, especially in the circle of Mayor Richard Daley and Chicago's Democratic machine, which had long opposed Rush and were impressed by Obama's audacity in challenging him.[46]

After a period of soul-searching and strategizing in the wake of his failed congressional bid, Obama chose a different stage for his political ambitions. To break out of Hyde Park and the South Side, he needed to deepen his connections to Chicago's white leaders. Beginning in 2001, Obama began to direct his energies toward Chicago's economic elite. Part of the reason was the redistricting of his state senate district to include parts of Chicago's wealthy "Gold Coast." His constituency, still diverse, was now whiter and richer. By the summer of 2002, when he launched his run to become the Democratic candidate for the U.S. Senate, his connections with Chicago developers and financiers became even more important. Running a statewide primary race (especially because one of his opponents was independently wealthy) required a huge campaign war chest. Obama continued to cultivate support in his Hyde Park district, reached out to traditional Democratic funders like trade unions, but also tapped wealthy developers, financiers, and attorneys by capitalizing on his Ivy League pedigree, his networking skills, and board service.

Obama's thickening web of connections among Chicago's elite—especially real estate developers, lawyers, and corporate executives—reflected his relationship to another important, if decidedly unromantic current in post-1960s urban politics. Many ambitious African American politicians—like their white and Latino counterparts—made their peace with policies that channeled investment dollars toward downtown redevelopment projects, such as office towers, convention centers, casinos, stadiums, and arenas. This reflected in part urban realpolitik: developers, corporate executives, and at-

torneys were among the most important campaign contribu-
tors in big cities like Chicago. But more importantly, Obama's
new relationships reflected his increasingly robust connection
to what urbanists called the "growth machine"—an alliance
of developers and investors who pushed for tax breaks and
public funds for large-scale urban redevelopment and used
their resources to bankroll political candidates who supported
their agenda. The evidence was mixed on the benefits of
the downtown development and gentrification projects that
the growth machine preferred. Entertainment venues like
stadiums attracted suburbanites and tourists to cities, but
often cost more in subsidies and tax abatements than they
earned. New construction projects created jobs—but in a
sector of the economy in which minorities were underrepre-
sented. Convention centers were a magnet for tourist dollars
and tax revenue and sometimes created service-sector jobs in
the hospitality industry. But few benefits of downtown redevelopment trickled down into predominantly African American neighborhoods—which in nearly every major city, including Chicago, witnessed steady disinvestment, even during the
boom years of the 1990s. Still, for cities eager to position
themselves as viable players in the national and world economies—as Chicago was—the lure of downtown development
and gentrification was irresistible.[47]

Chicago between the early 1990s and Obama's election as
president epitomized urban growth politics. Between 1995,
when the city engaged in a streetscape improvement project
in the Loop and surrounding neighborhoods, and 2006, when
the real estate market began to collapse, Chicago embarked on
an extensive program of government-subsidized urban redevelopment. It set into place tax incentives and other subsidies
to encourage investment in new office buildings and residential towers, condominiums, and townhouses. Gentrification,

especially on the North Side and near West Side, but even in Hyde Park (where real estate values skyrocketed), turned large sections of the city, once rundown and impoverished, into havens for urban professionals, wealthy retirees, cultural producers, and artists. With support from the Clinton administration, Chicago's public housing authority bulldozed the city's lakefront housing projects, opening up the cleared land for private sector development. On the North Side, the leveling of the massive Cabrini-Green public housing complex, which adjoined posh Lincoln Park, paved the way for gentrification, while displacing thousands of mostly black residents. But the benefits of urban redevelopment trickled down only into a handful of minority neighborhoods, mainly those clustered near the Loop and the University of Chicago. Overall, in the 1990s, the economic gap between Chicago's whites and its black and Latino populations widened. Neighborhoods on the North Side and lakeshore prospered, while vast swaths of the city, mostly in the South and West Sides, remained untouched by the infusion of capital. While black professionals revitalized sections of the city's storied Bronzeville neighborhood and gentrified the Oakland–North Kenwood neighborhood, other African American neighborhoods to the south and west continued to hemorrhage population and suffer disinvestment.[48]

Many of Obama's deep-pocket supporters were beneficiaries of the remarkable economic transformation of the city in the last decade of the twentieth century. Gentrification and downtown development generated real wealth in Chicago's FIRE (financial, insurance, and real estate) sector. There—as in most big cities—developers, the lawyers who represented them, and the bankers and mortgage brokers who provided capital became major political players. Like other ambitious politicians, Obama followed the money, relying on the support of wealthy developers and investors, among them hotel executive Penny Pritzker, real estate magnate Valerie Jarrett, billionaire Chicago developer and casino mogul Neil Bluhm, former civil rights lawyer and large-scale landlord Cecil Butler (whose holdings ranged from ravaged buildings in all-black Lawndale to posh lakefront condominiums), and pizza shop magnate and developer Antonin (Tony) Rezko (who helped Obama buy his $1.65 million Hyde Park house and the adjoining lot). Obama's alliance with Chicago's pro-growth elite was most visible in his staunch—and ultimately unsuccessful—support for the city's bid for the 2016 Summer Olympics.[49]

Obama also reached out to the city's black business leaders, even if their pockets were not as deep as those of the Loop's big financiers, developers, and attorneys. As a state legislator, Obama was especially attentive to getting lucrative state contracts for black businesses—whose executives in turn, provided financial support for his campaigns. As Valerie Jarrett recalled, when Obama was a state senator, he "insisted that they have an audience and then, to the extent that the state does business, the business the state does should reflect the diversity of our state." Whatever intellectual misgivings Obama had about Harold Washington's emphasis on "getting our fair share" gave way to a pragmatic acceptance of affirmative action in contracting. Here, too, Obama resembled the post-1960s generation of ambitious urban politicians who used public policies for the advancement of minority businesses, and who reaped at least modest political rewards for doing so. Black urban politics had its share of Moseses, Miriams, and Joshuas. It was infused by the rhetoric of civil rights. But its most successful and influential practitioners, including Obama, were pragmatists, not prophets, willing to make their peace with political players whom many civil rights and black power activists had vilified.[50]

While Obama developed his connections to Chicago's economic elite, he also faced a greater political challenge: his association with a predominantly minority constituency. Black politicians with ambitions to be elected by majority-white electorates, especially for statewide offices, face a major dilemma, namely, their association with "divisive" issues. In the eyes of the news media and the white public, black urban concerns were the embodiment of divisive. In addition, there was little self-evidently redemptive about urban politics—Chicago-style or not—despite the fact that it had been a vehicle for black advancement for decades. The deal making that was a constitutive part of urban politics was not a compelling story to tell on the campaign trail. Obama could not hold up the history of black coalition-building politicians as examples of his leadership or style, for most of them combined interracial outreach and race consciousness. As inspiring as their stories might be, few of them fit easily into a national narrative of civil rights and progress.

Obama faced a double challenge, especially as he set his sights on the U.S. Senate in 2004 and then, a few years later, the White House. He was at once a "historic" candidate—a black American making a serious move to the national stage. And, at the same time, he needed to persuade whites that he was different from the black public officials and spokespeople who had dominated the airwaves for decades. The art of electioneering is ultimately one of marketing and inspiration. And few politicians in recent American history have been more successful than Obama at inspiring his supporters. As Obama negotiated his way from Chicago politics onto the national stage—and as he built on the strategies of his predecessors, forging interracial coalitions and reaching out to the city's pro-growth elites—he refashioned his narrative of civil rights history, creating a powerful political persona, and at the same time reinforcing some of the most deeply cherished narratives about recent American history.

It is necessary to "transcend" the perception of particularism, group identity, and special interest issues to appeal to the widest constituency. That lesson, which Obama had first learned at Harvard, was indispensable to his political career. For a black politician hoping to win white support, speaking forcefully on any racial issue risked touching a political third rail. So as his political ambitions grew, Obama distanced himself from the black politicians who had paved his way by offering a generational critique of black political history, reiterating the conventional wisdom that "black politics is still shaped by the '60s and black power."[51] Over the course of the next decade, Obama grew increasingly critical of what he called the "fallout" of the 1960s, whether it be in the form of the "psychodramas of the baby boom generation" or in his description of his controversial pastor Reverend Jeremiah Wright, Jr., as "a child of the 1960s" who "often expresses himself in that language of concern with institutional racism and the struggles that the African American community has gone through." It was those "attitudes" and "grievances" that he suggested were anachronistic and unnecessarily divisive.[52]

As he recast his relationship to black politics and the 1960s, Obama did not, by any means, repudiate the history of civil rights—instead, he embraced a particular version of it, one that allowed him to synthesize his own identification with the Southern movement with his political ambition. As an aspirant to statewide and national office, Obama could not risk association with either its most principled or its most problematic practitioners, for even though whites professed color blindness, they remained skeptical of politicians whose rhetoric or style appeared "too black." By contrast, aligning himself with the history of the Southern branch of the civil rights movement was safe. The freedom struggle, once divisive, had become domesticated, transformed into a narrative of unity.

By the time that Obama began his electoral ascent, there was one figure whose history was no longer controversial, a figure untainted by the popular memory of racial polarization and division, who seemed to rise above ordinary politics—Martin Luther King, Jr. King cast a long shadow over American popular culture in late twentieth-century America. Since 1968, the news media had been engaged in a relentless search for the "next King," and many civil rights leaders jockeyed, none of them successfully, to become the single spokesman for black America. King's soaring rhetoric became the touchstone for black speech making. But most importantly, no black political figure (indeed no American historical figure of any background) was more widely accepted or admired.[53]

The transformation in King's image was remarkable. King had been controversial for his entire career. He was reviled in the South, and even Northern whites perceived him as the head of a movement that was pushing "too far, too fast." At the time of his death in 1968, he had become an outspoken critic of American capitalism and foreign policy. Unlike many moderate and conservative black leaders, King refused to denounce black power, even though he had expressed his misgivings about racial separatism. When advocates of law and order denounced the urban riots as an outbreak of lawlessness, King urged understanding. And when liberals urged King to stay on message, focusing on racial discrimination and civil rights laws, he instead railed against American involvement in Vietnam and called for a mass mobilization of poor people. Each of these positions lost King even some of his staunchest allies. By early 1968, his popularity had plummeted. But King's image was softened in the decades following his assassination.

King's metamorphosis from the man that J. Edgar Hoover considered "the most dangerous Negro in America" to a secular saint was complete by 1983, Obama's last year in college, when Ronald Reagan signed legislation naming the third Monday in January the Martin Luther King, Jr., national holiday. Although some remnant segregationists and Cold Warriors opposed the holiday on the grounds that King was an agitator or a Communist, he entered the canon of American heroes. His radical politics was largely forgotten in public discourse; he had become a wholly uncontroversial figure. King's transgressive message was reduced to its least unsettling components: King the patriot, who called America to be true to its timeless, founding values; King the antithesis of Malcolm X and black power; and King the moderate conciliator, who piqued the consciences of white Americans, nudging them gently along toward accepting the fundamental humanity of blacks. Conservatives, like Obama's Harvard classmates, reinterpreted King as a critic of affirmative action, despite the fact that from 1964 until his death, King consistently supported compensatory programs to provide opportunities for African Americans who had been, for generations, systematically deprived of economic opportunity. Only the rapidly shrinking labor movement and a handful of labor historians recalled King's steadfast support of trade unions.[54]

Lost, too, in King's rehabilitation was his scathing critique of white moderates, his call to all-out battle against materialism and privilege, and his demand for a "revolution in values." King's statement that "when machines and computers, profit motives and property rights, are considered more important than people, the giant triplets of racism, extreme materialism, and militarism are incapable of being conquered" resonated more with the fiery rhetoric of Obama's pastor, the Reverend Jeremiah Wright, Jr., than with the conciliatory language in Obama's own speeches.[55] It was a sign of changing times that King's lifelong mission of speaking truth to power transmogrified into a call for volunteerism and national service. Martin Luther King's dream had become a staple of school curricula—indeed by the end of the twentieth century, King topped the list of historical figures, including George Washington and Abraham Lincoln, familiar to American schoolchildren. He had become the founding father of a new, redeemed America.

Our conventional histories of King and the Southern freedom struggle reinforce a broader and still deeply held vision of American exceptionalism, one that relates civil rights to a timeless American political tradition, dating back to the founding, of equality and opportunity, what Gunnar Myrdal, author of *An American Dilemma*, called the "American creed." An emphasis on the Americanness of the civil rights movement effaces its roots in a deep current of black internationalism that shaped the politics of leading activists as diverse as King, Stokely Carmichael, and Malcolm X, inspired by the anticolonial struggles of mid-twentieth-century Asia, the Caribbean, and Africa. American civil rights activists were more likely to look to Mohandas K. Gandhi or Kwame Nkrumah or Frantz Fanon for models of activism and political organization than they were to seek inspiration from Thomas Jefferson or Thomas Paine or Eugene V. Debs. And an emphasis on the relation of the civil rights movement to American values of equality, opportunity, and rights overlooks the exclusionary, inegalitarian aspects of the American political tradition and ignores those who challenged it. The history of the black freedom struggle was simultaneously shaped by both an evocation of American egalitarianism and—just as powerfully—by a deep skepticism toward it.[56]

A regular at King Day events, Obama offered a fairly conventional take on King (one that would be echoed in the short-lived fracas during the 2008 Democratic primary between the Obama and Clinton campaigns over the role that King and Lyndon Johnson played in the civil rights legislation of the mid-1960s). In an opinion piece published in the *Chicago Defender* during his ill-fated campaign against Bobby Rush, Obama highlighted King's "willingness to maintain faith in the face of difficulty, to retain hope against all the odds." For Obama, the "passage of the 1964 Civil Rights Act, the 1965 Voting Rights Act, and the 1968 Open Housing Law are testaments to that faith. The proliferation of black elected officials throughout the Deep South, and the birth of the black independent political movement in Chicago grow out of the risks he took." Embracing King was, in part, a jab at his opponent's roots in black power politics, but more than that it reinforced a Whiggish narrative of civil rights history.[57]

It is a sign of how uncontroversial King had become that, in 2003, Obama launched his campaign for the U.S. Senate in a speech punctuated by the refrain: "What would Dr. Martin Luther King, Jr., say?" He portrayed King as the soft-spoken prophet of fairness, hope, opportunity, and an ill-defined change. "What we face today is more than just a deficit of dollars. We have a fairness deficit in this country. We have a hope deficit in this country. We have an opportunity deficit in this country," stated Obama. "And so I know what Dr. King would say, and so do you. He would say we have an obligation to our children and our country to stand up for a new direction."[58]

No moment was more important in the melding of Obama and King as national healers than Obama's widely acclaimed keynote address at the 2004 Democratic National Convention, which culminated with a call for national unity. "There's not a liberal America and a conservative America; there's the United States of America. There's not a black America and white America and Latino America and Asian America; there's the United States of America." Afterward, delegates and journalists alike compared the still mostly unknown Illinois state senator to King. Jesse Solis, a Latino delegate from Emporia, Kansas, shared a common reaction to Obama's entrance onto the national stage. "I went back in time. To me, he was like Martin Luther King. That's what impressed me about him."[59] Across the political spectrum, from conservative writer Amity Schlaes to *Chicago Tribune* columnist Clarence Page, pundits evoked Obama as the latter-day version of the consensus King, one whose message of hope appealed across partisan divides.[60] As Page wrote, "Obama is not a conservative, yet conservatives would be hard-pressed to find much in his speech with which to disagree. Well-crafted, it rose above the usual political pep talk to echo the all-American voice of liberal patron saint Martin Luther King Jr."[61] The *Denver Post* went further, wrenching Martin Luther King's oft-quoted line at the March on Washington out of context, arguing that Americans should be "judged by the content of their character, not the color of their skin," to hail both black leaders' supposed aversion to affirmative action. "Obama's eloquent address revived, for the Democrats, King's dream of a colorblind America. No racial quotas; no Jim Crow laws. Just Americans."[62]

Obama's power as an orator is his ability to seamlessly bring together—as he did at the 2004 convention, at Selma, and throughout his campaign for the presidency—his personal story with a narrative of national redemption. Obama read widely in civil rights history; he taught antidiscrimination law; and he steeped himself in the historical and scholarly literature on race, poverty, and inequality. This was a history that he knew better than all but a handful of Americans. But none of that history was particularly useful for an ambitious politician. Situating himself in a current of civil rights history that emphasized its radical currents would be political suicide. But there was something deeper than simple political instrumentality at work. During his journey through the polarized racial world of late twentieth-century America, Obama discovered his calling. It was to overcome the acrimonious history of racial polarization, whether it be black power or the culture wars—to act on the understanding that such polarization was anathema to national unity. As historians Lee Raiford and Renee Romano have written, since the 1980s, politicians, filmmakers, and opinion leaders have transformed "the memory of the movement as a tool of nation building." No one did so more than Obama.[63]

For Obama, as for all political leaders, history provides a scaffolding for politics: it is full of inspiration, examples, lessons, and analogies. The past can be used—and reinterpreted—for purposes of image creation, political mobilization, coalition building, and policymaking. Political actors create a useful past, sifting from it what resonates with their constituents, opinion leaders, and the general public, whitewashing those elements that are jarring and unsettling or inconvenient. And Obama did that with King. The history of the civil rights struggle—told through Moses and Joshua and King—was a historical theology, civic religion, a fundamentally Christian story of suffering, martyrdom, and redemption. King had cleansed America from its original sin of slavery; and Obama was his heir. By the time that Obama was inaugurated president, he had recast himself as an agent of national unification, one who could finally bring to fruition the few lingering, unmet promises of the civil rights movement.

Obama's power—as a candidate and as a president—has been his reappropriation for liberals of a unifying language of Americanism, one that, like all exercises in nation building, transforms history into the stuff of legend and poetry. From the cacophony of the recent past, from its messiness and tumult, Obama extracts a powerful, reassuring message of progress, a story as compelling as Ronald Reagan's evocation of the Puritan "city upon a hill" or Abraham Lincoln's reinterpretation of the founding creed of equality in his Gettysburg Address, both true and mythological at the same time. Thus Barack Obama's own quest for identity and the distinctive history of the black freedom struggle, of urban politics, of civil rights and black power, became the American story. What Obama called "my story" became "our story."

II

Obama and the Truly Disadvantaged:

The Politics of Race and Class

≋

In 1981, when Barack Obama, barely twenty, arrived in New York City, urban America had bottomed out. The civil rights marches of the 1950s and 1960s were a distant memory, and, despite the movement's hard-won victories, racial inequality seemed more entrenched than ever, especially in inner cities. The optimism that had infused the black freedom struggle gave way to a deep-seated pessimism about the intractability of urban poverty. Social scientists and journalists used a neologism—the "underclass"—to describe blacks and Latinos living beneath the poverty line in cities like New York, entrapped in what seemed to be a permanent state of impoverishment, characterized by long-term welfare receipt, family breakdown, chronic substance abuse, and crime, all traits that, like a hereditary disease, seemed to pass down from one generation to the next.[1]

It was impossible to escape the ravages of poverty in Obama's New York. The city had been ravaged by the fiscal crisis of the mid-1970s and bore the signs of massive public disinvestment, its unair-conditioned subway cars completely covered with graffiti, and its parks overgrown and strewn with trash, both the casualties of "deferred maintenance." Nearly every block in upper Manhattan was pockmarked by abandoned or terribly rundown apartment buildings and houses, the result of the gaps between high carrying costs and low rents. African Americans, Puerto Ricans, and Dominicans, all disproportionately represented in the ranks of the city's poor, lived crowded together in tenements and converted row houses, their once grand entrances often vandalized and their elevators in disrepair. Residents of unheated buildings used ovens or dangerous kerosene stoves to stay warm. Fires—the result of faulty wiring or spilled heating fuel or arson—were commonplace. Drug dealers worked the street corners with impunity; broken bottles and used syringes filled the gutters. Homelessness—the consequence of state and local disinvestment in mental health, the steady gentrification of single-room occupancy hotels, and the failed experiment in the deinstitutionalization of the mentally ill—was epidemic. And the city's racial atmosphere was poisonous, the result of sky-high crime rates, gang violence, everyday police brutality, and the bitter divisions wrought by the city's bloody battles over black power and its failed experiments in integration.

"I was seeing the steady fracturing of the world taking place," wrote Obama of his time in New York. "I began to grasp the almost mathematical precision with which America's race and class problems joined, the depth, the ferocity, of resulting tribal wars; the bile that flowed freely not just out on the streets but in the stalls of Columbia's bathrooms as well where, no matter how many times the administration tried to paint them over, the walls remained scratched with blunt correspondence between niggers and kikes." It is a bleak description of urban life at New York's—and Columbia's—twentieth-century nadir.[2]

This was a new world for the "skinny young man with a funny name" who had spent his adolescence at an elite private school in Hawaii and his first two years of college at Occidental, a wealthy institution in the suburbs of Los Angeles, distant from the grim realities of urban poverty. Obama described his journey through urban America in the 1980s as a search for his own personhood—a "sense of wholeness" that transcended the "bloodlines we inherited." But it was also an intellectual journey, one that led him to grapple with the most pressing social problems of his era, to develop an intellectual framework for thinking about race and class, and ultimately to adapt that vision to reflect his political ambition. It is a history of the personal and political coming together in ways that reflected a new understanding of race, poverty, and inequality in late twentieth-century America. It is a history, ultimately, of the political construction of race—of how Obama's response to racial inequality and that "steady fracturing" was shaped by his encounter with social science and social policy.

≋

Obama's urban education-still-in-progress and, in particular, his desire to resolve America's "tribal wars" led him to his calling: community organizing and racial justice. His brief stint canvassing college students at City College (one of the country's most racially diverse institutions) whetted his appetite for something more substantive. Radical activists and community organizers were a remnant, a fringe in Reagan's America, but the fact that they were beleaguered added to their zeal. New York's religious and leftist organizers led a nationwide mobilization against Reagan's foreign policy. In 1983, more than a million people marched in New York City for nuclear disarmament, the largest antiwar demonstration in American history. In 1984, canvassers hit the streets in Harlem, Bedford-Stuyvesant, Brownsville, and inner-city neighborhoods throughout the country, hoping to turn out black and Latino voters against Reagan. Even though the incumbent won in a landslide, 1984 witnessed the highest black turnout in a national election before 2008. For liberals and the Left—especially for those committed to civil rights—the grassroots mobilization in 1984 offered hints of dawn in what they considered to be midnight in America.[3]

After a brief and unsatisfactory career in corporate writing, Obama blanketed civil rights and community organizations with his résumé. Eventually he was offered a job in a city that he did not yet know—Chicago. There he would earn the equivalent of an advanced degree in urban policy—and develop a distinctive political framework for thinking about the intersections of race and class. Obama's experience in Chicago laid the groundwork for a racial and economic politics that fused community empowerment, Chicago School sociology, Clintonite social policy, and a religiously inflected ideal of racial uplift. Like all political fusions, it was riddled with tensions, but it helped position Obama to appeal to several divergent constituencies: the Democratic Party's intellectual Left; a bipartisan center that was completely overhauling welfare policy; and a rising black middle class committed to individual reform and racial uplift.

≡

No city better reflected and shaped the paradoxical realities of race in late twentieth-century America than did Chicago. Every major change that remade urban America was manifest, often in its most extreme form, in the Windy City. It was America's second most racially segregated metropolis (surpassed only by nearby Gary, and neck and neck with bitterly divided Cleveland and Detroit), the result of federal and local housing policies that balkanized the city into separate, unequal racial territories; discriminatory real estate and banking practices; and decades of block-by-block racial conflict led by whites who fought the "invasion" of blacks into their neighborhoods.[4]

The scars of urban transformation were everywhere. Chicago's once thriving black business districts had been bulldozed for urban renewal, replaced by the concrete canyons of expressways and the gargantuan blocks of modernist, highrise housing projects. Other neighborhood shopping districts, including the once-thriving Sixty-third Street corridor, just a short walk from Obama's Hyde Park home, were left for dead, ravaged by steady disinvestment. Metropolitan Chicago had also witnessed galactic suburbanization, sprawling for at least thirty miles in every direction into the prairie. Left behind were city neighborhoods with decrepit housing dating from the 1870s to the 1920s, much of it in dire need of repair. Many apartments were in the hands of absentee landlords, who milked the properties for what little they were worth. Chicago bore the scars of a struggle for racial equality that was still incomplete.

But Chicago was also home to one of the nation's most substantial populations of middle-class blacks—people whose hold on that status was, to be sure, tenuous. Among them were Frasier and Marian Robinson, who would become Obama's in-laws. Frasier was a pump operator in a city water plant; Marian a secretary. They were the beneficiaries of the civil rights struggle. Black Chicagoans had used a tool unavailable to their Southern counterparts for the first twothirds of the twentieth century: they leveraged the power of their votes to demand access to the jobs controlled by the city's Democratic machine. (Indeed, Frasier Robinson paid his dues as a precinct captain and, like many blacks, made a secure living in the public sector.) Jobs like Marian's in retail and banking had been almost completely closed to black women until the 1950s and 1960s, when groups like the Urban League successfully pushed for the placement of black women in clerical positions; after a decade of protest, both public and private employers in the region introduced controversial, but effective affirmative action plans that broke down the barriers of race in the workplace. By the mid-1970s, many selective institutions extended affirmative action to promising black high school graduates, especially those whose parents had gained precarious middle-class status, including the Robinsons' children, Craig and Michelle, both of whom attended Princeton.[5]

Michelle and Craig Robinson—because of extraordinary parental support—had made the best of Chicago's abysmal public schools. But they were the exception in an educational system plagued by overcrowded and rundown buildings, poorly trained teachers, out-of-date curricula, and staggering administrative costs. A long history of segregation, multiple-shift schools, white flight, and disinvestment created a legacy of institutional failure in Chicago. Chicago civil rights activists had pushed for equal funding and desegregation since the 1930s, but their efforts were rebuffed by the courts and by a creaking, recalcitrant educational bureaucracy. As a result Chicago's schools remained highly segregated by race in the post-1960s decades and were poorer than they had been before. And the environment in the surrounding neighborhoods was scarcely better. Even middle-class black neighborhoods, like the Robinsons' South Shore, lacked the basic amenities that suburban residents took for granted, like well-stocked supermarkets, clothing stores, and boutiques, even if there was no shortage of beauty salons, beer and liquor stores, and bars.[6]

Still, Chicago in the 1980s was a resilient place too, a thriving center of black culture in all of its diversity. It was home to a black media empire, which published *Ebony* and *Jet*. Its local black paper, the *Defender*, still one of the nation's best, had suffered the shifting fortunes of the press in the 1960s and 1970s (as with so many aspects of American life, African American institutions were, as sociologist Troy Duster once put it, canaries in the coal mine, the first to be afflicted by larger structural changes in the American economy). And culturally, the city still rode the glory of its once famous jazz and blues scenes, even if it was no longer the cutting edge of musical innovation, as were New York, Los Angeles, and Detroit.[7]

Chicago was also home to three of the most influential black clerics of modern times other than the Reverend Martin Luther King, Jr.: the Reverend Jesse Jackson, Sr. and his Operation Rainbow/PUSH; the Reverend Joseph Jackson (no relation to Jesse), who headed the National Baptist Convention until 1982; and Minister Louis Farrakhan, who inherited the small, but still-prominent Nation of Islam. (Jesse Jackson's headquarters, Joseph Jackson's church, and Louis Farrakhan's mansion were only blocks apart from each other—and all within walking distance of Obama's future Hyde Park home.) In the vast black neighborhoods that extended to the south and west, black churches, whether modest storefronts or megachurches, were the most visible neighborhood institutions and, in combination, served as important political actors. Chicago's black ministers played a crucial role mobilizing their members in local elections (most notably in Harold Washington's and Carol Moseley Braun's campaigns), and black churches were more likely to be politically engaged and to encourage political participation than were their white counterparts. In addition, many churches provided social services to neighborhood residents; and, regardless of their theological orientation, they provided a religious framework that permeated even ostensibly secular black activism in Chicago.[8]

Chicago also had a well-developed tradition of community and civil rights organizing. The center of the settlement house movement, popularized by Jane Addams's Hull House, the city had long attracted young idealists who hoped to transform its built environment and uplift its impoverished residents. Chicago's broad-shouldered industries had been the target of muckrakers and reformers. Beginning in the 1930s, Chicago had been one of the nation's centers of unionism. The city's two key industrial sectors—meatpacking and steel—had been colonized by two of the twentieth century's most powerful unions: the United Steel Workers of America and the United Packinghouse Workers of America. Both were among the few truly interracial institutions in the mid-twentieth century, and, even though they had blind spots (steelwork was rigidly segregated by race and ethnicity), they had records of allying with the struggle for black equality.[9]

Chicago had a long history of civil rights activism, especially around education and housing. Beginning in the 1930s, black women in Chicago spearheaded a campaign against the city's separate and unequal schools that culminated in a federal civil rights litigation, a massive school boycott, and citywide marches between 1962 and 1965. Chicago was also a bastion of the open housing movement. Its activists— Quaker and Communist, Catholic and Jewish, NAACP and CORE—fought against stiff white resistance to desegregate the city's public housing projects and battled, with few victories, against the high walls of racial prejudice in its suburbs, from blue-collar Cicero to upper-crust Deerfield. The Windy City had been, for a time in 1965 and 1966, the place where Martin Luther King, Jr., "took the movement North," in part because of its dense network of civil rights groups, many of which survived well beyond King's short stay there, still fighting against the odds. In the mid-1960s, Chicago had also become a major center of black power politics, with active chapters of the Black Panthers, the Young Lords, and the Deacons for Defense. By the late 1980s, Chicago was on the cutting edge of school reform politics, embarking on an experiment in community participation and parent involvement that was heralded by many as a powerful alternative to impersonal bureaucracy.[10]

Not surprisingly, given Chicago's history, Obama was attracted to three issues: labor, public housing, and education. And he gravitated toward a school of community organizing developed by one of twentieth-century Chicago's most influential activists, Saul Alinsky. A University of Chicago graduate, a leftist, and a lifelong agitator for social justice, Alinsky had pioneered the version of community organizing—developing indigenous leadership—that would become Obama's model. Ever pragmatic—he believed that the ends justified the means—Alinsky organized neighborhood residents to challenge aldermen, to fight for better jobs and schools, and to improve housing conditions. Alinsky's TWO (The Woodlawn Organization) had attracted activists from all over the country to its community development and job-training programs and had inspired community organizing efforts in places as far afield as Rochester, New York, and San Antonio, Texas.[11]

Barack Obama lived and worked in two separate worlds. During and after law school, he socialized with the city's black elite, visible enough that they earned the moniker "Buppies" (black urban professionals) in the 1980s. But it was the bleak, deindustrialized South Side and its left-behind residents who would ignite Obama's passion. On his first day as a community organizer, Obama stood outside the shuttered Wisconsin Steel plant on Chicago's far South Side. The "massive old factory," he wrote, stood there "empty and rust-stained like some abandoned wreck."[12] He recalled his boss and mentor, Jerry Kellman of the Calumet Community Religious Conference (CCRC), describing the workforce there. "All kinds of people used to work in the plant . . . Blacks. Whites. Hispanics. All working the same jobs. All living the same kinds of lives." Their livelihoods and their neighborhoods were now shattered, the casualties of a decades-long collapse of the steel industry, the result of trade policies that encouraged its globalization, beginning in the late 1950s. Kellman was right that workers of all kinds had toiled in the mills, but not all were affected equally. Until the 1970s, steel factories were balkanized by race, with black workers confined to the worst, most dangerous jobs and, usually, the first to be eliminated in financial hard times. Unemployment rates on the South Side were staggering, but especially among poorly educated black men who found few alternatives when the plants closed.[13]

Organizing on the South Side was difficult for Obama. He worked mostly alone and with a shoestring budget. Key to community organizing was building networks and trust—and both came hard to an outsider. "The first thing he did was listen to people, interview them one after another, and then look at notes," recalled Kellman. Obama took such copious notes that many of the people whom he encountered assumed he was working on short stories or writing a book. Meeting with church leaders and block organizers in Roseland, West Pullman, and Altgeld Gardens—South Side Chicago neighborhoods ravaged by disinvestment and unemployment—Obama undertook the task of listening to people's narratives and then working with them to figure out how to solve their problems. It was a collaborative process, helping ordinary people organize themselves.

The real challenge—and an insurmountable one for Obama and his cadre of Alinskyites—was dealing with the impact of Chicago's massive economic restructuring. It was a process that did not have solely local origins; the South Side was remade by investment decisions in brokerage firms in New York, London, and Tokyo and relocation decisions made in consulting firms and in suburban corporate headquarters. The flight of capital was rooted in interstate competition, as rural states, especially in the Sun Belt, lowered taxes and discouraged unionization to create a "favorable business climate" to attract companies from high-tax, high-wage cities like Chicago. Even more consequentially, Chicago and other old manufacturing cities were on the losing side of American trade policies that facilitated the emergence of cheap labor markets in Latin America, the Caribbean, and Asia.

Community organizers had the will but ultimately not the capacity to address these macroeconomic and political transformations. But they worked, at least, to mitigate their effects locally. Chicago's Alinskyites offered Obama both a diagnosis and a remedy for the city's economic woes. Kellman introduced Obama to one of the key principles in community organizing, one that would profoundly shape his protégé's politics. The CCRC, like many community organizations spawned in the last third of the twentieth century, emphasized the need for interracial coalition building, not out of a vague commitment to diversity or the notion that integration was uplifting, but because Chicago's economic transformations affected workers regardless of race or ethnicity. Kellman offered Obama an analysis of the process of deindustrialization as an economic transformation that did not respect the color line. Just as the packinghouse workers had argued that "black and white" should "unite and fight," to demand fair wages and decent working conditions, so, too, did the South Side organizers hope to forge a working-class majority to support job training and job creation programs.[14]

In 1980s Chicago, forging an interracial working-class alliance was, however, a nearly impossible task because of the city's long history of racial polarization and segregation. Black and white workers did not live in the same neighborhoods, worship in the same churches, or drink in the same bars. Their children did not attend school together. And they certainly did not intermarry—Chicago in the 1980s was no Hawaii. The result was deep suspicion across racial boundaries. Successful movement building depended on networks—and there were few everyday connections between black and white Chicagoans. Working with the Catholic Church, Obama and his fellow organizers succeeded in bringing together a small group of blue-collar Chicagoans across racial lines to lobby for a job bank program—and they succeeded, again quite modestly. Despite his commitment to interracialism in the long term, Obama directed more energy inward, organizing the black community itself. Blacks, he argued, needed to celebrate their "tribal affinities," and build a common identity from within, but only as a prelude to reaching outward and forging a "multicultural" coalition. Obama argued that "[a]ny African-Americans who are only talking about racism as a barrier to our success are seriously misled if they don't also come to grips with the larger economic forces that are creating economic insecurity for all workers—whites, Latinos, and Asians."[15]

Obama was modest about his accomplishments. "Sometimes I called a meeting, and nobody showed up," he recalled. "Sometimes preachers said, 'Why should I listen to you?'

Sometimes we tried to hold politicians accountable, and they didn't show up. I couldn't tell whether I got more out of it than this neighborhood." His biggest victory came in Altgeld Gardens, a segregated, low-income housing project. Going door-to-door, he found a small cadre of residents concerned about the deterioration of their buildings. Together they rented a bus and went to city hall to demand funds to remove asbestos. It was a small-scale effort—Obama did not join forces with other city groups working on similar environmental and public health issues—and fewer Altgeld Gardens residents joined him than he had hoped. But their efforts paid off.[16]

Even though Obama's experiences organizing on Chicago's South Side yielded few tangible results, they were formative for him intellectually and politically. He retained the Alinskyite commitment to cross-race coalition building and continued to see himself as a tribune for the "voiceless." Above all Obama kept his faith in grassroots community organizing as a tool for systemic change. Reflecting on his three years as an organizer, he called for "bringing together churches, block clubs, parent groups and any other institutions in a given community to pay dues, hire organizers, conduct research, develop leadership, hold rallies and education campaigns, and begin drawing up plans on a whole range of issues." In concert, the city's poor could overcome their powerlessness by pooling their resources and challenging politicians to be more responsive to community needs. In Chicago, that meant creating a pressure group that worked outside of the traditional channels of power—namely, the machine—but continued to focus on the narrow band of issues that could be solved at the city level. For Obama, black churches offered an example of the limits and possibilities of coalition building. As an organizer, he visited with dozens of South Side religious leaders—an experience that was both eye-opening and also depressing.

In 1995, he argued that "[a]ll pastors go on thinking about how they are going to 'build my church,' without joining with others to try to influence the factors or forces that are destroying the neighborhoods. They start food pantries and community-service programs, but until they come together to build something bigger than an effective church all the community-service programs, all the food pantries they start will barely take care of even a fraction of the community's problems."[17] Such neighborhood-wide organizations could effectively lobby for improved city services—not inconsequential gains on the micro level—even if they could never adequately address the macroeconomic changes that ravaged inner cities and their residents.

Obama's three-year stint on Chicago's South Side also instilled in him a realistic sense of the limits of self-help and community-based economic development and social services provision. Such programs faltered in the absence of more systemic reforms. The movement of which he was a part was the expression of an impulse that peaked in American politics after the 1960s: a belief in the virtue of local control and community self-determination. The devolution of power to community groups and localities was reinforced by federal policies, beginning in Lyndon Johnson's War on Poverty and accelerating under Nixon's "New Federalism" and Community Development Block Grant program, meant to supplant large-scale federal urban investment with assistance to community development organizations and nonprofits. Like most reform impulses, community control had unintended consequences. Perhaps the most significant, which Obama recognized, was that efforts to empower the poor risked reinforcing the notion that urban problems and their solution were ultimately the responsibility of inner-city residents themselves, not of the larger society. In 1988, just as he wrapped up his three-year organizing stint, Obama wrote that community-based development projects "can and have become thinly veiled excuses for cutting back on social programs, which are anathema to a conservative agenda." Obama's observations, coming after nearly a decade of sustained federal disinvestment in cities, were astute. In 1980, the federal government provided 12 percent of city budgets; ten years later, the figure had fallen to 3 percent. Chicago, with a black mayor and a still-formidable Democratic Party machine, was particularly unpopular among Washington's Republican leaders and suffered greatly from federal spending cuts during the Reagan and Bush years. Obama saw that legacy on the streets of the South Side every day. It would take more than asbestos remediation and job banks to transform the lives of Chicago's working-class and poor.[18]

≡

The communities that Obama had attempted to organize were even poorer and bleaker in 1991, when he returned to his adoptive hometown after finishing law school. "Upon my return to Chicago," he wrote, "I would find the signs of decay accelerated throughout the South Side—the neighborhoods shabbier, the children edgier and less restrained, more middle-class families heading out to the suburbs, the jails bursting with glowering youth, my brothers without prospects." For three years, Obama had been cloistered at Harvard, and there is no indication that his legal education there was formative for his understanding of urban inequality and poverty. But his new intellectual home, the University of Chicago, would be. The university had long attracted scholars doing cutting-edge work in law, economics, and sociology (each discipline had its own influential "Chicago School"). For twelve years, beginning in 1992, Obama taught courses on civil rights, voting rights, and due process, but he kept his distance from the law school's distinguished faculty, seldom attended talks and faculty seminars, and made few close friendships there. Chicago's strength in the fashionable field of law and economics attracted scholars somewhat to Obama's right (the most influential being Richard Posner, appointed a federal judge by George H. W. Bush), but there is no evidence of their impact on Obama. Instead, he remained an enigma to his colleagues, avoiding controversy and committing none of his legal ideas to print. "He figured out, you lay low," suggested Richard Epstein, a fellow faculty member and a well-known, right-leaning libertarian. In the classroom, Obama likewise maintained a studied impartiality, seldom tipping his ideological hand, even regarding controversial topics like electoral redistricting, affirmative action, and criminal procedure. If there is any clue to Obama's intellectual proclivities, he seemed to be attracted to Chicago faculty—in both law and economics—who were politically liberal, but who occupied a disciplinary middle ground. His closest colleague was law professor Cass Sunstein, a prominent advocate of "judicial minimalism" (focusing on a narrow reading of cases, unencumbered by sweeping legal principles), deliberative democracy (advocating the civil airing of divergent points of view), and, most recently, incremental modification of individual behavior (in contrast to efforts to mandate social change). And Obama befriended his future economic policy adviser Austan Goolsbee, an MIT-educated scholar of taxation and regulation, whose version of neoclassical economics was well within the mainstream of the profession, even if he was to the left of many of his quite conservative departmental colleagues. Neither Sunstein nor Goolsbee had much to say about race and public policy, though it is likely that their regulatory gradualism (emphasizing incremental policies over sweeping legal change or structural economic transformation) influenced Obama. To a great extent, Obama's thinking about race was shaped by the third Chicago School—the one based in its sociology department.[19]

The University of Chicago, its faculty, and its students dwelled at a remove from the city around them. The Rockefeller-built campus, with its somber architecture, arranged into collegiate gothic quadrangles, stood apart from the pedestrian grit of the city, distant from the rumbling El. Hyde Park was also something of a peninsula, cut off from the grubby Woodlawn neighborhood to the south by what had been the midway of the 1893 Chicago World's Fair, and bounded on the east by Lake Michigan. In the 1950s, the university further isolated itself from the bleak industrial city and insulated itself from the black migration (or what Chicago School sociologists called "neighborhood succession") that was remaking large swaths of the South Side. The university's president and trustees supported the large-scale urban renewal projects that evacuated many black residents from nearby neighborhoods, and at the same time promoted investment in Hyde Park and Kenwood to attract faculty and maintain middle-class status. Many of the streets to the north of the university, bordering North Kenwood and Oakland, end in cul-de-sacs, part of 1950s and 1960s antiblight efforts, meant to cordon off Hyde Park from the surrounding communities.[20]

The university's sociology department, by contrast, remained both in and of the city. Since the 1910s, Chicago School sociologists had used the city as a laboratory to explore questions of race, ethnicity, and urban space. Early in the century, Robert Park (a former journalist turned social scientist), Lewis Wirth, and Ernest Burgess developed a powerful ecological theory of urbanism, analyzing the connections between ethnic, racial, and economic stratification and the geography of the city. Challenging biological determinism and racial essentialism, the Chicago School sociologists emphasized the environmental origins and spatial manifestations of stratification, delinquency, and social disorganization. The combination of the ethnographic and ecological, the micro and the macro, attracted an extraordinary cadre of graduate students and researchers to the university, among them E. Franklin Frazier, St. Clair Drake, and Horace Cayton, some of the most important black social scientists of the twentieth century.

In the heyday of the Chicago School, faculty and graduates did not draw a bright line between their scholarly pursuits and engagement with the opportunities and problems of their city. They joined reform organizations, collaborated with settlement house workers, provided advice to community and civic groups, and consulted for local foundations. Hundreds of master's and doctoral students produced theses and dissertations on just about every aspect of life in Chicago's black, working-class, and ethnic neighborhoods. They studied civic institutions, visited political clubs, drank in neighborhood bars, chronicled street gangs, and worshipped in ethnic churches, all in service of their ethnographic research.[21]

The Chicago School's influence waned between the 1950s and the 1970s, but its star was on the rise again by the time that Obama began working as a community organizer. In 1972, the university had hired a young, relatively unknown black sociologist, William Julius Wilson. Hiring Wilson was a bit of a gamble for a hidebound institution like Chicago, with relatively few black faculty members and, despite its location, a small number of black students. Wilson lacked the Ivy League credentials, the European pedigrees, the Chicago degrees of most of the university's faculty. But the gamble more than paid off. Wilson's 1978 book, *The Declining Significance of Race*, was a rare scholarly study that won both academic acclaim and a wide nonacademic readership. Provocatively, the book argued that the civil rights legislation of the 1960s had restructured black America, creating what he considered to be an unprecedented gulf between the black poor and the expanding black middle class. Wilson argued that civil rights advances had benefited one segment of black America (giving them more and more common ground with whites), while systematically disadvantaging workers and the poor, whose plight worsened in the decade after the passage of the Civil Rights Act of 1964. Quietly Marxisant in its orientation, *Declining Significance* highlighted a theme that would recur in Wilson's later work, namely, an emphasis on the impact of economic restructuring on workers across the color line.[22]

As one wag put it, had Wilson called the book "The Increasing Significance of Class," it would not likely have made the splash that it did. In the increasingly conservative 1970s, when economic analyses of racial inequality were slipping to the margins, when the civil rights movement seemed to be waning, and when national attention turned to the controversial policy of affirmative action, Wilson's book resonated not because of its economic framework, but instead because of its reassuring message that the United States was, to a great extent, overcoming its long history of racial division. Wilson's book coincided with a national debate about affirmative action (the same year it was published, a badly divided Supreme Court upheld the use of racial preferences in higher education in its *Bakke* decision). Wilson offered an alternative to the divisive racial politics of the late 1970s—one that resonated with Obama's own experience as a community organizer: push parochial racial concerns, including affirmative action, to the side, and instead create an interracial coalition to demand industrial reinvestment and job creation.[23]

Soft-spoken and consummately professorial, Wilson became a controversial figure. Advocates of affirmative action and racial integration argued that Wilson overstated the impact of civil rights laws on the everyday patterns of racial segregation and underestimated the persistence of discrimination. Wilson's book, they feared, would provide sustenance for what Daniel Moynihan had called a period of "benign neglect" of racial issues. And in the ever more conservative climate of the late 1970s, they feared that still-fragile black gains would be rolled back, leading to a period of resegregation and worsening racial inequality.

Obama was drawn to Wilson—even if many black South Siders were skeptics. Among numerous black intellectuals, including Obama's soon-to-be minister and spiritual adviser Reverend Jeremiah Wright, Jr., Wilson was notorious. In fact, Wilson's name came up in Obama's very first meeting with Wright at Trinity United Church of Christ. Obama recalled Wright referring to those "miseducated brothers, like that sociologist at the University of Chicago, talking about 'the declining significance of race.' Now, what country is he living in?" Although Obama found himself attracted to Wright's church, in part because of its "powerful program, this cultural community, one more pliant than simple nationalism, more sustaining than my own brand of organizing," Wilson appealed to his intellect.[24]

Wilson's most important and influential book came out during Obama's stint as a community organizer on Chicago's South Side. *The Truly Disadvantaged*, published in 1987, was sweeping and synthetic, elegantly weaving together problems often considered separately from each other into an overarching theory of urban inequality. Using black Chicago as a case study, Wilson highlighted the devastating impact of deindustrialization, offering evidence that jibed with Obama's hands-on experience.

Wilson also offered a largely impressionistic argument about the bifurcation of black Chicago by class. In his view, the withdrawal of the middle class from impoverished inner-city neighborhoods had deprived the black poor of their leavening influence. Under segregation, Wilson contended, middle-class and poor blacks shared the same neighborhoods and attended the same churches and schools. As a consequence, middle-class blacks served as role models and created what he called "social buffers" against the effects of economic dislocation. All of that changed in the post-1960s years, in his view. Middle-class flight, argued Wilson, left Chicago's poorest neighborhoods—already beset by deindustrialization—ravaged by the loss of social and cultural capital, their residents socially isolated from "mainstream society." Affirmative action and desegregation, he argued, had the unintended consequences of reinforcing poverty. It was an interpretation of class division that resonated especially among middle-class blacks who looked upon black urban poverty with a sense of guilt and harked back to the segregated communities of their parents' generation with more than a bit of wistfulness.[25]

Obama found this argument so compelling that he singled it out in his 1988 article on community organizing. The young activist was coming to terms not simply with his own racial identity, but with his class position, straddling the black and white worlds, and the two black South Sides, separate and unequal. At the time, Obama did not comment on Wilson's third set of arguments—which emphasized the cultural impact of concentrated urban poverty on family structure and marriage patterns, though he would return to those themes later in his career.[26]

With the publication of *The Truly Disadvantaged*, Wilson set the agenda for a generation of social scientists concerned with urban poverty and the "underclass." Wilson's influence extended well beyond the academy, because his arguments resonated, for different reasons, with liberal advocates of equality and conservative critics of the black family. *The Truly Disadvantaged* became one of the central texts informing the soon-to-be-raging debate about welfare reform. Wilson's book—like some of the most enduring works in the social sciences—was, like the Bible, open to multiple readings. (Wilson, who remained at core an economic structuralist, lamented what he considered to be misunderstandings and misuses of his arguments.) Left-liberals found Wilson's unsparing depiction of the ravages wrought by deindustrialization to be the book's landmark contribution. Conservative readers also found sustenance in Wilson's work, although he was a staunch critic of such Reagan-era interpretations of poverty as those of Charles Murray, who blamed an overgenerous welfare state for exacerbating poverty and providing "perverse incentives" that discouraged work and marriage. But Wilson's revitalization of the controversial Moynihan Report—and his emphasis on family dysfunction and breakdown in inner-city neighborhoods—reinforced conservative arguments about the cultural and behavioral origins of poverty (even though Wilson, like Moynihan, insisted that social disorganization was a consequence of the transformation of urban labor markets, not its cause). For nearly twenty years, the Moynihan Report had gathered dust—criticized for "blaming the victim" and for reinforcing racist arguments about the black "matriarchy." Wilson eschewed the characterization of black families as matriarchal, but he uncritically accepted one key element of Moynihan's framework—namely, his emphasis on men as breadwinners and women as caregivers. Moynihan and

Wilson alike emphasized the impact of economic transformations on men's labor force participation, ignoring black women's place in the urban economy. Like Moynihan, Wilson attributed family breakdown instead to the debilitating effects of unemployment and underemployment on the marriageability of young African American men.[27]

Obama found himself in between the two worlds that Wilson chronicled: the gritty world of the "urban underclass" and the city's diverse black middle class. He interacted with first-generation strivers like the Robinsons; socialized with young black professionals (lawyers, physicians, and executives) who had attended elite universities, often as beneficiaries of affirmative action, and who constituted a small but growing segment of the city's elite; and worshipped with the left-leaning members of the bourgeoisie and middle-class nationalists in the pews at Trinity UCC.

Wilson's arguments about class—his explanation of urban poverty and his lament about the dissociation of the black middle-class and poor—had a lot of commonsense appeal, especially among uprooted black professionals who looked back, often with a sense of nostalgia and loss, at the supposedly tight-knit communities of their parents' and grandparents' generations. Paraphrasing Wilson, Obama worried that "middle-class blacks are leaving the neighborhoods they once helped to sustain." But, unlike some black professionals who found suburbia attractive, Obama remained committed to the city. "I'm not interested in the suburbs," he told an interviewer in 1990, in a rare unguarded moment. "The suburbs bore me." For Obama, the fate of poor, black South Side neighborhoods and places like his own interracial, increasingly well-off Hyde Park were intertwined—and the "catalyst for redevelopment throughout the South Side" would be "middle class residents who are energetic and invested in the community."[28]

Nostalgia for the "old neighborhood" where middle-class residents uplifted the poor and sustained a sense of community was more a symptom of the distortions of memory than an actual description of everyday life under segregation. Urban historians debunked the notion of a "golden ghetto" of cross-class collaboration and social control that informed Wilson's work and Obama's concern about black middle-class flight. Wilson ignored the everyday class conflict in the segregated cities of the early and mid-twentieth centuries; and exaggerated the impact of civil rights on housing segregation, which remained the norm for poor and better-off blacks alike in the late twentieth century. Middle-class blacks clung tenaciously to their prosperity; their children often experienced downward mobility; they had substantially less wealth than did their white counterparts; and because of high rates of racial segregation, they mostly lived in communities with inferior schools and infrastructure and high crime rates, never very far physically or psychologically from the black poor. Ethnographers found that one of the defining characteristics of black middle-class households—in sharp contrast to those of whites—was their high likelihood of having a family member living in poverty.[29]

The gap between the black middle class and poor was not as wide as Wilson had surmised. But the perception of that gap shaped Obama's worldview. And it became a central element in his evolving politics. Wilson's other key argument—the need for interracial coalition building around a shared politics of class—resonated just as deeply with Obama. It validated his work as a community organizer and his understanding of the history of the civil rights movement. It became the central theme in Obama's political vision. In 1995, Obama chastised those who "believe that the country is too racially polarized to build the kind of multiracial coalitions necessary to bring about massive economic change." It was a theme that he reiterated as often as possible on the national stage, notably at his 2004 address to the Democratic National Convention, and in his political memoir, *The Audacity of Hope*. There, Obama distilled Wilson's argument in five pages, arguing for economic policies that "may have little to do with race at all," but will benefit minorities and whites alike. "An emphasis on universal, as opposed to race-specific programs," he argued, "isn't just good policy; it's also good politics." Wilson confirmed Obama's instinct that, despite the obstacles, coalition building was a political necessity.[30]

≡

Very few politicians, especially those successful on the national level, cling to a single position. Their views are, by necessity, protean, shaped in response to political currents, the needs and demands of their constituents, and their sense of the times. Barack Obama's views on race and inequality were very much in transition in the mid-1990s, as liberal intellectuals, analysts, and politicians systematically grappled with the tangled relationship of race, class, and liberalism. It was a liminal period for Obama, then making his first bid for office.

One moment, during his first campaign for the Illinois State Senate, captures Obama's shifting position on race, class, and inequality. In early 1996, Chicago's chapter of the Democratic Socialists of America sponsored a forum on economic insecurity. Obama and Wilson addressed a crowd of several hundred. Obama offered a Wilsonian riff on the politics of welfare reform in the mid-1990s, calling for policies "to create productive communities," through what the DSA's rapporteur, in a close summary of Obama's words, called a combination of "the best instincts of the conservatives with the better instincts of the left." For Obama, the root cause of poverty was a lack of "human capital" in the inner city—a theme that dated back to work on "manpower" development in the 1960s, but which Wilson, among others, had revitalized in the 1990s. To that end, Obama put forth an agenda that advocated greater spending on schools and job training.[31]

Obama's entry into electoral politics coincided with the passage of the most sweeping federal welfare legislation since the War on Poverty. The Personal Responsibility and Work Reconciliation Act of 1996 was the strange fruit of a quarter century of conservative challenges to the legitimacy of welfare and the previous decade of foundation-sponsored, liberal scholarship shaped profoundly by Wilson's emphasis on the fusion of culture and structure. The postwelfare program that it created, Temporary Assistance to Needy Families (TANF), brought to fruition an argument launched by conservatives in the late 1960s that welfare was the major cause of poverty because it incentivized family breakdown, discouraged work, and fostered an unhealthy culture of dependency. In the last third of the twentieth century, Republicans had played on white voters' anxieties about economic insecurity by highlighting their fears of an undeserving black poor. At the same time, conservative think tanks developed blueprints to roll back regulation, weaken civil rights enforcement, unravel affirmative action, and dismantle as much of the New Deal and Great Society as was politically feasible.[32]

The rightward thrust on race, regulation, and the welfare state prompted soul-searching among liberal intellectuals and politicians. Foundations, policymakers, and politicians engaged in an intense debate about "targeting" and "universalism," questions with both normative and practical import. Normatively, liberal political theorists grappled with the question of redistributive social democracy, namely, the particular form of the American social welfare state. Scholars in political science, sociology, and, to a lesser extent, history revived an old question: why is there no socialism (or why is there no European-style social democracy) in the United States? Their answers varied, but to a great extent they converged on a set of explanations that emphasized the political costs of America's politics of difference: the difficulty of building political will for redistributive programs in a racially and ethnically divided nation.[33]

At the same time, politicians, pundits, and policy analysts confronted the rightward turn in American politics and began drafting blueprints for a new Democratic majority. The debate about liberalism and its travails played out in the pages of influential periodicals like the *New Republic*, the *New York Times*, and the *Washington Post*. Liberal journalists like Thomas and Mary Edsall, Mickey Kaus, Jim Sleeper, and Michael Tomasky argued that the Democratic Party had lost its appeal on the national level because of backlash against the social programs of the 1960s, including affirmative action. Hardworking Americans were alienated by costly welfare expenditures that seemed to reward indolence. Exacerbating the Democrats' woes, in their view, was the party's capitulation to "identity politics." Black power radicals, aided and abetted by white leftists, alienated well-meaning, color-blind, working- and lower-middle-class whites and drove them from the New Deal coalition. The "lesson" from this history was clear: so long as the Democrats were captive to "special interests" (namely, minorities), they would never be a majority party on the presidential level. Democrats, in this view, needed to distance themselves from civil rights activists and flamboyant black political leaders like New York's Reverend Al Sharpton and the Reverend Jesse Jackson. And, more importantly, Democrats had to accept—in its fundamentals—the conservative critique of the welfare state.[34]

The most influential voices in the debate about Democrats, welfare, and racial politics came from the Democratic Leadership Council (DLC), a business-oriented reform caucus that embraced a softer version of many Republican policy initiatives. If the Democrats wanted to win back the support of Reagan Democrats—those white, Rust Belt voters who rejected the party of FDR because of their anger at urban crime, unwed motherhood, welfare, and taxes—they would have to embrace the politics of "tough love" toward the poor. The Democrats had to recover the moral high ground from the GOP by echoing its calls for personal morality and individual responsibility. That meant making welfare recipients work, expanding the prison system and implementing stiffer penalties (including capital punishment) for crime, and replacing race-based affirmative action with color-blind initiatives.[35]

While the DLC advocated a rightward shift on both cultural and economic policies, other Democrats to their left, most of them sympathetic to organized labor, advocated a revival of a class-based politics that they believed had kept the New Deal coalition glued together until the 1960s. They took a different lesson from the history of the Democratic Party's post-1968 woes: namely, that the Democrats suffered by prioritizing race over class, cultural issues over economic concerns. Among them was Wilson who—building on the arguments of his first two books—called for a class-based politics that emphasized common economic grievances in place of a divisive politics of racial difference. To that end, Wilson weighed in on the side of "universalism" rather than "targeting." For Wilson, this meant implementing what he called a "hidden agenda" that would "improve the life chances of groups such as the ghetto underclass by emphasizing programs . . . [to] which the more advantaged groups of all races can positively relate." The key was adopting technically "race-neutral" social programs that would disproportionately benefit minorities because of these groups' overrepresentation among the working-class and poor.[36]

The Clinton administration took advice from both camps. During his campaign for the presidency in 1992, Bill Clinton, a longtime DLC member, distanced himself from Jesse Jackson, criticized black rapper Sistah Souljah, and refused to stay the execution of mentally retarded Arkansas convict Ricky Ray Rector, all gestures to placate culturally conservative white voters. At the same time, however, he consulted with Wilson and other major scholars of poverty policy (for example, David Ellwood, a Harvard economist who had also conducted research in Chicago, whom he would hire to design his welfare reform policy) and supported—at least in principle—the notion that the solution to urban poverty was transforming the labor market. By the mid-1990s, the Clinton administration had distanced itself from the controversial policy of affirmative action ("mend it, don't end it"), supported work requirements and wage supplements in lieu of traditional welfare ("make work pay"), and argued for programs targeted toward "working families" rather than toward the poor, including the earned income tax credit.[37]

Obama recoiled at Clinton's cultural conservatism (he called the Sistah Soujah incident "clumsy" and the Rector execution "frighteningly coldhearted"). And he was also skeptical of Clinton's efforts to reach across the aisle and fashion social policies that appealed to conservatives. "On the national level, bipartisanship usually means Democrats ignore the needs of the poor and abandon the idea that government can play a role in issues of poverty, race discrimination, sex discrimination or environmental protection," Obama argued in a 1996 interview in a University of Chicago student newspaper. While Obama was, at first, ambivalent about welfare reform, over time he adopted his own version of Clintonian triangulation, offering qualified support for affirmative action and endorsing welfare reform, while advocating for the expansion of job training and child care programs, transportation subsidies to smooth the welfare-to-work transition, and the EITC. As Obama moved onto the national stage as a first-term U.S. senator, he moved further toward Clinton, voting to reauthorize welfare reform and publicly celebrating Clinton's emphasis on morality and personal responsibility. As he wrote in 2006, "conservatives—and Bill Clinton—were right about welfare as it was previously structured."[38]

≡

Obama's position on welfare, class, and race continued to evolve in the late 1990s—shaped deeply by his assimilation into Chicago's black bourgeoisie. The call for personal responsibility in the mid-1990s resonated with Republicans and Clintonite Democrats alike. But it also found a favorable hearing in an unexpected quarter, among urban African Americans themselves. Blacks were the most loyal Democrats, and by most measures they were on the party's left, but their views on many social issues dovetailed rather more closely with those of conservatives than most commentators acknowledged. On one hand, polls showed that African Americans believed in overwhelming numbers in a federal safety net for the neediest, and in compensatory programs for those affected by discrimination. But on the other, African Americans were, in the aggregate, suspicious of welfare, skeptical about dependency, and strongly supportive of self-reliance. Religious blacks, like their white counterparts, were especially critical of what they considered to be dysfunctional attitudes toward marriage, sexuality, and the family. If social scientists drew a sharp distinction between structural causes of urban inequality (joblessness, discrimination, segregation) and individualist explanations (the lack of a work ethic, bad parenting, illegitimacy, and drug use), many urban African Americans fashioned explanations that blurred the two together.[39]

As his connections with Chicago's black bourgeoisie thickened, Obama grew more comfortable with a syncretic politics of personal responsibility and social action. In her book *Black on the Block*, sociologist Mary Pattillo brilliantly describes the contact between "the truly disadvantaged" and the "black bourgeoisie" on the streets of Chicago's gentrifying North Kenwood neighborhood (just north of Obama's home). There, black urban professionals, gentrifying a poor inner-city neighborhood, simultaneously attempted to "uplift" their impoverished neighbors by serving as role models, but also by using their political and economic clout to improve everyday living conditions. They thought about poverty in both intimate and structural terms. What Pattillo calls "black middlemen" fused a politics of respectability with engagement in local and national politics to improve the position of the black poor. It was a late twentieth- and early twenty-first-century version of an old theme in black elite activism.[40]

It is a position riddled with tension—at once social democratic and paternalistic—but one that helps to explain Barack Obama's evolving racial politics. The position was one reinforced at community meetings, in everyday discussions at barbershops and over kitchen tables, and especially in church. To understand Obama's analysis of race, poverty, and policy requires spending a little time in that most controversial venue, the Reverend Jeremiah Wright's Trinity United Church of Christ. There, whether or not Obama attended services frequently (he claims to have missed many of Wright's most polemical sermons), he was introduced to a distinctive version of black theology, one that defied easy categorization as leftist, liberal, or conservative.

It was all three, all at once, in ways that few observers, because of their fixation on some of Wright's most inflammatory rhetoric, recognized. Wright drew from the tradition of "black liberation theology," a current of religious expression that combined black power's emphasis on racial pride, the civil rights movement's critique of discrimination, inequality, and militarism (one especially visible in the late sermons of Martin Luther King, Jr.), and a profoundly moralistic critique of personal dysfunction and individual sin. Wright was uncompromising in his criticism of racism; he lambasted the exclusion of women from leadership positions in the church; he called for black churchgoers to support people with AIDS; he advocated a living wage and denounced corporations like Wal-Mart; and he criticized U.S. foreign policy in Africa— all positions that brought him allies on the left. Wright also excoriated the Clinton administration's "messed up welfare-to-work bill."[41] But Wright was also consistent in his call for self-help. Black youth, he preached in 1994, "got to start taking responsibility for the stuff we are doing to ourselves."[42] It was a theme that he reiterated—especially when addressing black men. His ministry's emphasis on self-discipline, group pride, and what he called "the black work ethic" led him to sometimes call his listeners to turn inward, or, as he exhorted, "while we can't change the world, we can certainly change our house."[43]

While public policy advocates often drew sharp distinctions between individual-level interventions and social solutions, Wright's ministry embodied the syncretic character of black religious thought—one that took different forms in different congregations—but one with conservative elements that befuddled mainstream media commentators, most of whom were unfamiliar with black religion, downplayed its nuances, and lacked a language to describe a politics that does not easily correspond to the conventional binaries of left/right, integrationist/separationist, or black power/civil rights. Obama himself reinforced this point in his 2008 Philadelphia speech on race, reminding his audience that Wright's theology could not be boiled down to his controversial, prophetic statement, "God Damn America." Obama spoke of a "quintessentially American—and yes, conservative—notion of self help" that "found frequent expression in Reverend Wright's sermons."[44]

Wright's emphasis on racial pride, self-help, social service, and middle-class responsibility to the poor shaped Obama's own version of poverty and policy. As he became increasingly prominent, Obama began to preach the gospel of personal responsibility, in addition to advocating for job creation programs and the EITC. "When you're African American or a minority of any sort, you can always find an excuse not to succeed," he said in a 2005 interview, "Nothing is easier than being able to excuse your lack of accomplishment on race or poverty. What is challenging, but ultimately most fulfilling, is recognizing that, although we don't choose the world we're born into, we still have a responsibility to make something of it."[45] Obama hammered home the themes, especially in speeches to predominantly black audiences, first in Selma, Alabama, in 2007; later at Ebenezer Baptist Church at a Martin Luther King Day celebration; again in a celebrated Father's Day speech at Chicago's massive Apostolic Church of God in 2008; and in his address to the one-hundredth-anniversary conference of the NAACP in July 2009.[46]

Again and again, Obama reiterated a theme utterly familiar to black churchgoers, but surprising to white audiences—namely, that the first step toward racial equality was black folks lifting themselves from poverty through self-discipline:

turning off the TV, respecting their elders, pulling up their pants, and working hard. In particular, he singled out black men. At Apostolic, he lamented that many fathers "have abandoned their responsibilities, acting like boys instead of men. And the foundations of our families are weaker because of it." Obama was not alone in making these arguments publicly. His political rival, Congressman Bobby Rush, roused his black constituents by preaching a mix of black empowerment and up-by-the-bootstraps self-help. "Government will never liberate us," preached Rush in 2003. "We have to assume a lot of that responsibility for ourselves, and I don't see Congress or elected office as being a cure-all for our problems. . . . Ultimately, you've got to make up your mind to change yourself." Echoing similar themes, comedian Bill Cosby and onetime black power advocate turned Harvard psychiatrist Alvin Poussaint penned a best-selling self-help book, *Come on People*, in which they offered up a mix of racial romanticism ("in the 1950s, we feared our parents and respected them"), libertarianism ("Governments don't care. People care, and no people like parents do"), and hoary parental advice ("Turn off the TV," "Reinforce Standard English," and "Respect Our Elders"). Some black leaders—among them Jesse Jackson—worried about Obama's airing the "dirty laundry" of the black community; and many whites heard Obama's call for personal responsibility as a courageous act, evidence that Obama had transcended the politics of racial grievance, and was willing to stand up and speak the hard truth to his own people.[47]

But Obama's call for individual responsibility was neither new nor risky. He had heard it in countless conversations in Chicago. In *The Audacity of Hope*, he wrote: "In private— around kitchen tables, in barbershops, and after church— black folks can often be heard bemoaning the eroding work ethic, inadequate parenting, and declining sexual mores with a fervor that would make the Heritage Foundation proud."[48] Black churchgoers nodded at Obama's familiar admonitions and most applauded. One of the major themes in late nineteenth- and twentieth-century African American history has been the importance of the politics of uplift (the special role that middle-class blacks play in "lifting as they climb," that is, serving as role models and moral guardians for their poor and working-class brothers and sisters). Embracing "middle-class" values was an essential first step toward full acceptance of the race by whites. Calls for uplift and respectability have animated the careers of countless black ministers, community activists, and intellectuals. Obama's convictions on the matter of self-discipline and self-help cannot, however, be separated from his political agenda. Unlike Wright, who voiced his call for self-help from the pulpit of a black church, or Cosby, who wrote a self-help book intended for a black audience, Obama intended white voters to listen; this was part of his appeal to the culturally conservative voters whom the Democrats had spent the best part of twenty years trying to win back. It was an echo of Clinton's calls for personal responsibility, but all the more powerful because it seemed to be (and was) more than a transparent political ploy. White commentators heard Obama tell his "own people" to shape up and whiten up; journalists remarked on the novelty of Obama's message and his candor. The reason that Obama's call for responsibility seemed new was that the everyday world of black politics and religion remained—and remains—invisible to most of white America.

≋

By 2008, Obama had developed a patchwork quilt of social politics, one that combined left-leaning calls for cross-class alliance building, Clintonite advocacy for the end of welfare as we knew it, and a Christian moralism that allowed him to build an unlikely bridge between black churchgoers and culturally conservative whites. It was—as with so many of Obama's key positions—a synthesis of deep currents in American political and intellectual life in the last third of the twentieth century. Each component of that synthesis was familiar, but the combination of all of them together amounted to something that not only put Obama in the mainstream, but allowed him to fashion a political appeal, at once, to left, center, and right; to blacks who called for a combination of social justice and personal responsibility, to whites who believed that the roots of black poverty lay in individual behavioral and moral failings, to Democrats who had worked to create a new liberalism that combined a jobs-oriented economic populism with cultural conservatism, to those right and center who supported the bipartisan efforts to reform welfare, and to those on the left who were uncomfortable with it. It is a political fusion that succeeds—as do most—by allowing Obama to remain, as he noted in the opening pages of *The Audacity of Hope*, "a blank screen on which people of vastly different political stripes project their own views."[49]

III

"A More Perfect Union"?

The Burden of Race in Obama's America

≋

On November 4, 2008, about two hundred thousand people gathered in Chicago's Grant Park. The faces in the crowd—white, black, Latino, and Asian—all waving little American flags—embodied Barack Obama's vision of an interracial America, one that he had so eloquently presented just eight months earlier in Philadelphia, in the defining speech of his political career. There Obama offered Americans a way past the nation's deepest divisions—calling for a "more perfect union" to overcome the nation's deepest-rooted divisions through a shared sense of purpose.[1]

Smaller celebrations erupted spontaneously in many Chicago neighborhoods. In Puerto Rican Humboldt Park and Mexican Pilsen, fireworks went off and crowds gathered in restaurants and bars to cheer the president-elect. Despite prognostications during the primaries that Latinos would be hesitant to support an African American presidential candidate, Mexican American votes in the Mountain West and Cuban and Dominican American votes in Florida were decisive to Obama's victory. Students in Hyde Park took to the streets, as they did in college towns around the country, cheering

Obama's victory. The celebrations in Chicago's white neighborhoods were more subdued. The home state favorite won overwhelmingly among whites in Chicago and in many of its wealthier suburbs (Obama made his biggest gains over his Democratic predecessors among wealthy white, suburban voters)—although nationwide only 43 percent of whites voted for Obama (2 percent more than had pulled the lever for John Kerry in 2004).[2]

The most enthusiastic Obama celebrations were, no surprise, in the city's vast black neighborhoods, most of them distant from Grant Park. On the South and West Sides huge crowds gathered, literally dancing in the streets; cars packed with cheering youth honked their horns and shouted out their windows; and some revelers fired shotguns into the air to celebrate. Nearly every barbershop and salon, restaurant, and corner store in black Chicago was bedecked with Obama posters (months later, many of them remained up); street vendors hawked T-shirts with the new black Trinity (Martin, Malcolm, and Barack); and photographs of the Obama family graced many storefront windows. Never in American electoral history had black voters turned out in such numbers or so unequivocally. Black votes were not decisive in Illinois—but blacks' unprecedented turnout gave Obama the edge in several closely contested states, including once-Red North Carolina, Indiana, and Virginia. The very iconography of Obama—and his place in the pantheon of black heroes— suggested that the president-elect meant something quite different on the South Side from what he meant elsewhere. He had become the embodiment of black consciousness, a symbol of the race.[3]

Election night in Obama's Chicago manifested the city's extraordinary diversity (and, for that matter, America's). But the city's very geography, its division into racial and ethnic enclaves that have remained stubbornly resistant to change, also reflects the paradoxes of race in modern America. By a rough measure, the crowd at Grant Park reflected Chicagoland's multicultural demographics. But the disparate neighborhood celebrations represented the patterning of race on the metropolitan landscape. And after the parties were over, those who had gathered to cheer Obama returned home in a city whose everyday life is still indelibly shaped by race. Since the 1920s, metropolitan Chicago has been a balkanized territory, especially by black and white. When Obama arrived there as a community organizer a quarter century ago, Chicago was at the top of the list of most segregated metropolitan areas in the United States—and it is still near the top today.[4]

But all is not the same: Chicago, like so many major (and minor) American cities, was transformed by the most important demographic phenomenon of the last four decades: the reopening of immigration to the United States. The largest city in the Midwest, Chicago had long been a second-tier destination city for newcomers from Latin America and Asia. By 1990, however, the city entered the ranks of ports of entry, and in the next decade, it bucked the trend of its declining Rust Belt neighbors: it gained population, largely because of the enormous influx of immigrants. By 2000, 22 percent of the city's population was foreign born. Almost half of Chicago's new immigrants were Mexican; about a fifth were Asian, including Indians, Filipinos, Vietnamese, Chinese, and Koreans. The city became an emblem of a polychromatic, polyglot America. And none of these new immigrant groups were as racially segregated as blacks.[5]

Barack Obama—himself the son of an immigrant—embodies the paradoxes of race, ethnicity, and identity in modern America. In Obama's Chicago—and in the racially and ethnically complex America of the last four decades—America's past and its uncertain future collide. On one side is a hyper-segregated, majority-white nation; on the other, projections of a majority-minority nation, a place where the old binaries of race no longer hold. Some futurists contend that by 2040, America will be a brown-hued nation, its once dominant European-descended population blended into a new whole. Others look toward a postracial America where intermarriage and intermixing will destroy the "ethnoracial pentagon," which rigidly classifies all Americans as African, Asian, Latino, Native American, or white. Not all are optimistic. The growing trends of class inequality, combined with persistent segregation, have led some to foresee a United States that resembles Colombia or Brazil, places of extraordinary diversity in color, where everyday interracial contact is commonplace but where a still deeply entrenched color hierarchy economically and socially disadvantages those of African descent. Any one of these prognostications may be correct, but history offers no good way to assess their probability, other than the chastening lesson that the vast majority of past demographic and economic predictions, especially those made with great certainty, have proved to be wrong.[6]

But it is clear that whatever the future brings, race relations in the present are in a state of flux, characterized by a mix of continuities and discontinuities. Racial optimists, those who believe that the United States is becoming a postracial society, and racial pessimists, those who posit that the nation is entrapped in a deep-rooted, even timeless history of racial oppression, are both right and wrong, for history is seldom linear and the future is unpredictable. Scientific and social scientific understandings of race, public opinion about race, and the lived experience of race are ever changing: they are shaped by their cultural and political contexts. It is now axiomatic in the social sciences that race is a social, cultural, and political construction, one that takes on different forms and meanings in different periods of history. But history plays a role in the definition and meaning of race at any given moment, for notions of blackness and whiteness, of Asian as a racial category or Latinos as *la raza*, are shaped by past definitions and, more importantly, by the way that those definitions shaped institutions and the rules that govern them. The results can be paradoxical. In the early twentieth century, for example, assumptions about the biological inferiority of blacks led actuaries and real estate economists to develop housing policies that mandated the official segregation of housing and mortgage markets. Those actuarial standards were abandoned in the 1960s, as a consequence of shifting racial attitudes, pressure by civil rights groups, and local, state, and federal laws forbidding discrimination in the real estate market. But housing segregation patterns—which resulted in the first place from assumptions of racial inferiority—remained deeply entrenched for decades afterward. It is possible, as sociologist Eduardo Bonilla-Silva has argued, to have "racism without racists" or, put differently, public policies that have origins in racism and which perpetuate racial inequality but are no longer justified in explicitly racial terms.[7]

The history of the late twentieth century—and the early twenty-first—is shaped by tensions between a historically specific postracial framework, a now broadly accepted discourse of color blindness that has especially deep appeal to whites, and a still deeply rooted racial consciousness, especially among African Americans. Two other racial frameworks coexist with these—a white identity politics that dares not speak its name, and a sensibility toward racial hybridity that shapes the worldview of many new immigrants and, increasingly, a younger generation of white and black Americans. Racial ideas and practices, especially on the individual level, are contested and evolving, perhaps more rapidly now than at any time since World War II. But ideas about race matter most in their context, and all of them—color blindness, racial consciousness, and hybridity—play out in a racialized geography, polity, and economy, whose contours are deeply rooted in the twentieth century, where the distinctions of black and white are still not only relevant but often decisive. The past is still a heavy burden on the present.

≡

Let's begin with the microcosm and move outward from there. That microcosm is Chicago. There the new realities of immigration and ethnic diversity have proven to be profoundly disruptive of our traditional understandings of race; but, at the same time, recent demographic and economic shifts in key respects have reinforced some of the deepest-rooted patterns of racial separation and difference.

In the fall of 2006, around the time that Obama began to lay the groundwork for his presidential campaign, William Julius Wilson and University of Chicago sociologist Richard Taub published a study of race and ethnicity in Chicago, entitled *There Goes the Neighborhood*. In it, they offer a sobering view of a city where ethnic groups look with suspicion across the invisible boundaries that mark urban turf. Wilson and Taub conclude that "neighborhoods in urban America, especially in large metropolitan areas like Chicago, are likely to remain divided, racially and culturally." It is a depressing prognosis that reflects the distance Wilson has traveled from his once strongly held position that racial distinctions were waning in post–civil rights era America. But it also corresponds with the findings of social scientific researchers—and increasingly historians—about the complex relationship of post-1964 immigration to the questions of race and identity in the modern United States.[8]

The book's most important and troubling finding is that when it comes to their perceptions of African Americans, whites and Latinos are more alike than different. Mexican newcomers in Chicago, for example, quickly learned to view blacks as shiftless and prone to crime. In one Chicago neighborhood, Hispanic and white residents formed an alliance to prevent the busing of their children from the neighborhood's overcrowded schools to nearby, mostly black schools. In another, Mexican American residents, many of them recent arrivals, expressed their contempt for blacks, whom they saw as competitors for scarce resources. As a consequence, Chicago has the highest rate of black-Hispanic segregation in the United States.[9]

Chicago is not unique. The nation's largest and most ethnically diverse metropolitan areas, New York and Los Angeles, have experienced similar patterns of interracial hostility and segregation. In Los Angeles, Harvard political scientist Lawrence Bobo and University of Pennsylvania demographer Camille Charles found that newly arriving Asian and Latin American immigrants—while they have a complicated relationship with the white majority—quickly define themselves as "not black." They are attracted to predominantly white neighborhoods and, like whites, view the presence of even a modest number of blacks as a sign that a neighborhood is troubled or in decline.[10]

The new immigration has—despite an outburst of nativism unparalleled since the anti-immigrant crusades of the early twentieth century—destabilized racial categories, though unevenly. The most pronounced reshuffling of the racial deck involves those new Americans of Latino and Asian descent; change has been slowest for Americans of African descent, even those new immigrants from places as diverse as Liberia, Senegal, Haiti, and the Dominican Republic. The Latin American immigrant experience is instructive. For the last thirty years, as tens of millions of Spanish-speaking immigrants from Central and South America and the Caribbean have flooded into the United States, anti-immigrant commentators have fretted about the Latinization of the United States and the emergence of an unassimilable minority. But such fears have proved ungrounded. Despite their incorporation under antidiscrimination and affirmative action laws as a racial minority beginning in the 1970s, and the ongoing efforts of civil rights advocates to protect the rights based on that status, ordinary Latinos have resisted efforts to organize as a racial group because of the diversity of Latino national origins, the incommensurability of racial categories between Latin America and the United States, and the embrace of the category "white" by a majority of Latin American immigrants and their children.[11]

When the U.S. Census Bureau introduced the category "multiracial" in the 2000 census, most observers expected it to reflect the growing number of black-white marriages. Instead, the vast majority of those who checked more than one box selected some Latin American identity and "white." By contrast only 2 percent of self-identified whites and 4 percent of self-identified blacks considered themselves as being of more than one race. By nearly every measure, Latinos of non-African descent (a crucial distinction) have amalgamated to a degree comparable to that of southern and eastern European immigrants in the early twentieth century. Rates of intermarriage between Americans of Hispanic and non-Hispanic European descent are up to one-third in aggregate; and they rise in each generation removed from the first wave of entrance to the United States. And despite such publicized comments as George H. W. Bush's reference to his grandchildren (whose mother is Mexican American) as "little brown ones," data show that mixed-race children of Latin American descent, with no visible African heritage, are regularly viewed as "white."[12]

The instability of racial classification is even more striking when it comes to the groups that are broadly labeled Asian American. There are variants within and between groups, but overall the experience of Asian immigrants since the 1960s inverts the racial order that prevailed as late as the 1940s, when Chinese and Japanese were forbidden to emigrate to the United States, when public health authorities advocated their quarantine, and when many (especially the Japanese) were even prevented from owning property. It is impossible to generalize about Americans of Asian descent: Hmong, Laotian, and Filipino immigrants, for example, have faced greater obstacles than have Indian, Chinese, and Korean newcomers; many of the former groups come from impoverished backgrounds, while many of the latter arrive in the United States with capital and relatively high levels of educational attainment. But even accounting for variations between ethnic groups and the fact that most Asians are new arrivals to the United States, more than one-quarter of all married people of Asian descent in the United States have a non-Asian partner (87 percent of these partners are white). For married people of Japanese American descent, up to 70 percent have a partner who is not Asian.[13]

Immigration patterns have also transformed urban and metropolitan geographies in ways that confound traditional racial categories. Most big cities have Chinatowns, and many have Mexican Villages or their equivalent. Smaller groups are clustered in Japantowns, Little Koreas, and Filipino neighborhoods, especially in older western cities. But more than half of new immigrants to the United States since the 1990s live in suburbs; the result is an extraordinary diversification of what had been, fifty years ago, some of the whitest places in America. And patterns of segregation vary widely from group to group. Asian communities—especially those that are portals for the newest immigrants—remain somewhat concentrated (and those patterns vary by group), but overall less so than those of Latinos. Latino segregation varies by group as well—South American immigrants are the least segregated; Afro-Hispanics (such as immigrants from the Dominican Republic) the most segregated. But overall, the pattern tends toward residential amalgamation, with the noteworthy exception of African-descended immigrants.[14]

By nearly every measure, African Americans stand alone. The most persistent manifestation of racial inequality in the modern United States has been racial segregation in housing and education. From 1920 through 1990, patterns of black-white segregation hardened in most of the United States, despite shifts in white attitudes about black neighbors, and despite the passage of local and state antidiscrimination laws and the enactment of Title VIII of the Civil Rights Act (1968) which prohibited housing discrimination nationwide. There was slight improvement in the last decade of the twentieth century, mostly in and around military bases, college towns, and new exurbs in the Sun Belt with no extensive history of racial hostility, and with metropolitan or regional governments. That those places desegregated to some degree was a reminder of the powerful role that government policy and the structure of local governments could play in undermining racial segregation: the military is the largest substantially racially mixed institution in the United States; colleges and universities institutionalized diversity through affirmative action; and metropolitan governance discouraged segregation because whites lacked the opportunity to jump across municipal boundaries for towns with better schools and public services, while leaving minorities behind.[15]

By contrast, in metropolitan areas with fragmented governments and school districts, overwhelmingly in the Northeast and Midwest, racial segregation rates have remained particularly high. The reasons are varied, but they reflect the long-term effects of discriminatory patterns that date to the early twentieth century. Before that, in most places—North and South—blacks and whites lived in relatively close proximity. Real estate brokers refused to rent or sell houses to blacks in white neighborhoods, actuaries determined that a neighborhood's racial composition was the most important factor in measuring property values, and whites began to resist black incursion, sometimes with violence. And federal pro-homeownership programs, beginning in the New Deal, wrote discriminatory provisions into public policies. The result was that during the mid-twentieth century, expectations about the racial composition of neighborhoods were established that proved extraordinarily resistant to change.[16]

After the 1968 Fair Housing Act, real estate agents developed more furtive tactics to preserve the racial homogeneity of neighborhoods. The most significant was "steering," that is, the practice of directing white home buyers to all-white communities and black home buyers to predominantly black or racially transitional neighborhoods. Real estate brokers catered to what they believed were the prejudices of their white customers. Audit studies of housing discrimination conducted by the Department of Housing and Urban Development and by local housing and nonprofit agencies, where matched pairs of black and white "testers" are sent to randomly selected real estate offices, consistently show the persistence of discriminatory treatment of black home seekers and renters. And more recently, studies have shown stark racial differences in access to mortgages and loans—leaving minority neighborhoods especially devastated by the collapse of the real estate market that began in 2006 and accelerated rapidly during the "Great Recession" that began in 2008. Discrimination continues to play a significant role in dividing housing markets by race. When house hunting or loan shopping, blacks simply do not have the same degree of choice as do whites.[17]

Persistent residential segregation compounded educational disparities. Beginning in the late 1970s, when courts began a thirty-year process of abandoning the mandate of *Brown v. Board of Education*, school districts around the country resegregated by race, especially by black and white. In the North—where *Brown* was never wholly enforced, and where white mobility thwarted integration—blacks witnessed some educational gains in the 1960s and 1970s, notably a narrowing of test-score gaps with whites. But schools resegregated n the period between the 1980s and the early twenty-first century and the test-score gap leveled off.[18] The process of educational resegregation has accelerated most recently in the South, where the Civil Rights Act of 1964, Department of Education intervention, and court-ordered busing led to enormous shifts in racial patterns in the late 1960s. Since the late 1990s, however, metropolitan-wide school desegregation plans have been rolled back by federal courts that have declared districts "unitary"—that is, racially balanced. A good example is Charlotte, North Carolina, where a 1972 Supreme Court ruling led to a metropolitan-wide busing plan. By the 1980s, Charlotte had one of the most integrated school districts in the country, and racial gaps in achievement narrowed. That experiment in integration ended in 2001, and considerable resegregation followed. Most recently, in the 2007 *Parents Involved* case, the conservative majority on the Supreme

Court struck down as unconstitutional (using the color-blind rationale) voluntary school desegregation programs in Louisville, Kentucky, and Seattle, Washington, and threatened similar programs elsewhere. Education research has shown consistently that majority-minority schools face one of several problems: they are underfunded by comparison to schools in nearby majority-white districts; they face high teacher turnover; they are more likely to have outdated facilities and classroom materials; and, most significantly, their students tend to be disproportionately poor, lacking the familial resources and the cultural capital to do well in the classroom.[19]

It is important to note that black-white residential segregation by race is not—and has not been—a natural consequence of disparities in income between blacks and whites. Middle-class and wealthy blacks are only slightly more likely to live near whites than are poor blacks. In an examination of the thirty metropolitan areas with the largest black populations in the United States, sociologists Douglas Massey and Nancy Denton found no significant difference in the segregation rates of poor, middle-class, and well-to-do African Americans. "Even if black incomes continued to rise," write Massey and Denton, "segregation would not have declined: no matter how much blacks earned, they remained racially separated from whites." The most recent census data reaffirm that regardless of income, African Americans, in the aggregate, remain residentially segregated, and that the differences in rates of segregation between blacks of high and low socioeconomic status remain modest.[20]

African Americans are far more likely than whites to be economically insecure. The statistics are grim. In 2006, the median household income of blacks was only 62 percent of that of whites. Blacks were much more likely than whites to be unemployed (black unemployment rates have remained one and a half to two times those of whites since the 1950s), in part because of workplace discrimination. Data from the Russell Sage Foundation's Multi-City study of Urban Inequality show that in Detroit, Boston, Atlanta, and Los Angeles, many employers make hiring decisions on the basis of stereotypes about minorities, and use race or ethnicity as "signals" of desirable or undesirable work characteristics. Social scientists have documented employers discriminating against job applicants with comparable credentials when one has a "black" name or has a place of residence in a known "black" neighborhood.[21] Even more significant, blacks are still most likely to live in areas that have been left behind by the profound restructuring of the national and international economy, notably in major cities in the Northeast and Midwest. The suburbanization of employment—but not of minority housing and transportation—has further hindered black job opportunities. As a result, nearly one-quarter of all American blacks, but only one in ten whites, live beneath the poverty line.[22]

The starkest racial disparities in the United States are in wealth (a category that includes such assets as savings accounts, stocks, bonds, and especially real estate). In 2003, the U.S. Census Bureau calculated that white households had a median net worth of $74,900, whereas black households had a median net worth of only $7,500. It is here that the burden of history is the greatest. Census surveys and social scientific studies have documented an enormous gap in asset holdings between blacks and whites, largely because of differences in holdings in real estate, the only significant asset that most Americans own. Blacks are still less likely to own their own homes. Even in 2005, at the peak of the most recent real estate bubble, only 49 percent of blacks owned their own homes, compared to 74 percent of whites. And because of persistent racial segregation, the value of homes that blacks own is significantly lower than that of white-owned homes. Racial differences in homeownership rates and disparities in real estate values and household assets have devastating long-term effects. Whereas many whites can expect financial support at crucial junctures in their lives (going to college, getting married, buying a home, paying for a medical emergency), the vast wealth gap means that blacks cannot. The wealth gap also affects intergenerational transfers. A majority of whites can expect at least modest inheritances as the result of their parents' accumulated wealth, but few blacks can expect such good fortune.[23]

Not surprisingly, blacks have been disproportionately affected by market failures in home financing and personal credit from the New Deal through the early twenty-first century. From the 1930s through the late 1960s, blacks seldom had access to federally backed mortgages and loans; in that period and beyond, they were more likely to buy properties using expensive nonmortgage instruments like land contracts; and beginning in the 1980s and 1990s, as the Reagan, Bush, and Clinton administrations deregulated the financial, personal loan, and mortgage markets, predatory lenders (from pawnshops to payday loan agencies to subprime mortgage brokers) found their most lucrative markets among minorities. In 2006, more than half of subprime loans went to African Americans, who comprise only 13 percent of the population. And a recent study of data from the Home Mortgage Disclosure Act found that 32.1 percent of blacks, but only 10.5 percent of whites, got higher-priced mortgages—that is, mortgages with an annual percentage rate three or more points higher than the rate of a Treasury security of the same length. The result has been growing economic insecurity among African Americans, even those of middle-class status.[24]

Another important indicator of quality of life is health. One's long-term expectations are shaped in fundamental ways by one's experience with illness, injury, and death—from the care of a sick child or adult, to the economic impact of disease and disability, to the devastation of seeing a family member die, particularly in an untimely fashion. The racial and ethnic gaps in health and life expectancy are stark. The life expectancy of whites in 2004 was 78.3; for blacks, it was 73.1. The life expectancy gap between black men and white men was particularly large: white men can expect to live 75.7 years; black men can expect to live only 69.5 years.[25]

Racial gaps in health—closely correlated with poverty—are significant throughout the life course. In 2003, infant mortality rates were nearly 2.5 times as high for blacks as for whites. The rates were highest in impoverished central cities. Blacks have significantly higher death rates than whites for most of the top ten leading causes of death in the United States. Throughout the life course, blacks are more likely than whites to die of homicide, residential fires, drowning, and pedestrian accidents. The gap in homicide rates is enormous. Black men have a rate of death by homicide nearly seven times that of white men; the homicide rate for black women is nearly six times that of white women. The gap between black and white homicide death rates is greatest among young men; homicide is the leading cause of death for black men between the ages of fifteen and forty-four. The grim reality of violence affects large segments of black America, not merely the poor. A recent study found that a remarkable 70 percent of blacks surveyed stated that they knew someone who had been shot in the last five years, more than double the rate for whites. The racial differential in crime explains only part of the final significant racial gap—and the one that has grown vastly in the last decade as a result of a bipartisan effort to expand the carceral state. Black men are eleven times as likely as whites to be in prison. The effects of imprisonment, even for a short term, have devastating long-term consequences. Those who have served jail time are far less likely to find remunerative work and suffer all sorts of related social dislocations over their lifetimes. [26]

≣

These troubling statistics give the lie to any notion that America is fundamentally postracial. But they were seldom discussed during the 2008 campaign season, except by John Edwards in his short-lived run for the presidency. Even though Barack Obama had spent part of his career as a civil rights attorney and had a long track record of grappling with racial issues as a community activist and legislator, his advisers feared that he would be branded as a "special interest" candidate, or as a racial firebrand who would discount the interests of the majority, if he raised issues of racial disparities and inequality on the campaign trail. As a result, in 2007 and 2008, Obama seldom spoke directly about race except when he was asked directly about it.

Of course, when it came to Obama's candidacy, few political commentators kept silent on race. It ran like a black thread through the Democratic primaries and the general election, most generally in the form of comments about the historic nature of Obama's campaign, his nomination as the first African American presidential candidate by a major party, and his decisive victory. Racial issues—usually in simplified form—animated much political punditry. During the Democratic primaries, Obama faced criticism (largely fueled by a handful of media commentaries, rather than by any trend in public opinion one way or the other) that he was "too white" to win the support of black voters, an argument that grew from the seeming paradox that many prominent black politicians supported Hillary Clinton's candidacy for the Democratic Party nomination. The notion that Obama was "too white" for black voters had fleetingly risen during the 2004 senatorial race in Illinois, but was belied by polls and election returns alike, just as it was again in polls as early as February 2007, during the lead-up to the Democratic primaries. Racial prognostication took a different form during the furor that followed reports that Obama had described white working-class voters as "bitter." In this view, Obama was "too black" to win over the blue-collar voters who had been long perceived as a crucial swing vote. Both views were impressionistic, rather than based on hard data. The notion that Obama was "too black" for blue-collar whites was put to rest by data from the 2008 election showing that white voters in the lower-income categories supported Obama by margins greater than they had John Kerry in 2004 or Al Gore in 2000.[27]

Racial tensions briefly flared again, when Obama supporters accused primary opponent Hillary Clinton of racial insensitivity when she credited Lyndon Baines Johnson with the passage of the 1964 and 1965 civil rights legislation, rather than highlighting the role of Martin Luther King, Jr. During the tense South Carolina primary, Obama's campaign charged former president Bill Clinton with fueling racial division by comparing Obama's campaign to Jesse Jackson's runs in 1984 and 1988. And during primaries and general election campaign, explicitly racist campaign literature, rhetoric, and gestures gained widespread media attention. The Internet was flooded with racialized caricatures of Obama, arousing the anger of liberal bloggers. For days, the blogosphere was alight with materials like a California Republican Party flyer depicting Obama surrounded by a watermelon, fried chicken, and ribs, or a high-level Republican operative's recording of a song entitled "Barack the Magic Negro," to the tune of "Puff the Magic Dragon."[28]

But for all of the minor racial squabbles—and even the vile racism that crept into the campaign—what was more striking in 2008 was the ubiquity of the rhetoric of color blindness among Democrats and Republicans alike. After the tense primary in South Carolina, Obama supporters roused the huge crowd at the victory celebration with the chant "Race doesn't matter! Race doesn't matter!" For their part, Obama's opponents went to great lengths to distance themselves from even the suggestion that they race-baited on the campaign trail. And only a small percentage of those who did not vote for Obama claimed that they did so on grounds of race. In their comprehensive analysis of election results, political scientists Andrew Gelman and John Sides found that Obama's race was more likely an advantage with voters than a disadvantage.[29]

By huge majorities, voters professed—echoing the chants at the South Carolina victory party—that race didn't matter. The ubiquity of color-blind rhetoric is testimony to the effectiveness of more than a half century of civil rights activism in delegitimating overt, public expressions of racial prejudice. In the North through the 1950s and for at least another decade in the South, it was commonplace for whites to use racial epithets in public meetings, in letters to elected officials, and in interactions with blacks in public places. While there are still unrepentant racists who shout "Nigger" or draw cartoons depicting African Americans—including Obama—as simians or worse, or hang nooses to intimidate blacks, those incidents are far less common than they were a half century ago and their consequences far less severe.

Even more consequential has been the dramatic decline in the number of whites who, by any measure, express racist sentiments overtly. By the 1960s, polls and public opinion surveys showed that whites professed to view blacks and whites as alike beneath the skin. Growing majorities answered "no" to questions that measured racial prejudice, including whether or not they would mind having black neighbors or sending their children to racially mixed schools. By the 1970s, a majority of Southern whites no longer professed their support for official Jim Crow laws. By 2007, a statistically improbable 87 percent of whites claimed to have black friends. It became de rigueur for whites to profess color blindness.[30]

It might be that their expressions of color blindness are disingenuous. Some neuropsychologists, for example, suggest that racial prejudice is deeply rooted in the subconscious. Survey researchers suggest that whites have been cued to avoid expressing racist sentiments, even when they still hold them. Uncovering persistent racism required devising subtler questions to detect bias. Some sociologists contend that color-blind rhetoric is just a smoke screen to provide a patina of legitimacy to still deeply engrained racism. But however real, superficial, or spurious color blindness is, the ubiquity of color-blind rhetoric has profoundly altered the ways that politicians and policymakers talk about race. Obama saw the opportunities presented by color-blind rhetoric, but was also constrained by its limitations.

As the belief in color blindness gained traction in the last third of the twentieth century, a new set of explanations emerged to explain the persistence of racial separation and inequality. Racial segregation no longer carried the force of law; it was no longer the product of irrational prejudice. Rather racial inequality was a natural consequence of race-neutral market forces. Like lived with like. Any remaining segregation was the sum of countless individual choices about where to dine, where to shop, where to live—choices that reflected group affinities. This explanation had an element of truth to it, which made it all the more plausible. Segregation was, in part, the consequence of individual decisions about where to live, based in part on a healthy sense of communal identity (including the preferences of some blacks for the comfort and familiarity of all-black communities), and in part on rational choices about the quality of schools and municipal services. But this view rested on three faulty assumptions: that blacks and whites alike had unrestricted choice about where to live, that housing markets were unaffected by the legacy of past policies that had racially discriminatory impacts, and that the disparities between municipalities and school districts had nothing to do with race, even though the best-provisioned communities invariably had few black residents.

Color blindness had another, more benign manifestation. A corollary to the decline in overt racial expression—the positive side—was to be found in professions and performances of antiracism. Just as color-blind rhetoric took hold, whites began to defensively recoil at charges of racism. In the 1940s, when civil rights activists emphasized the anti-American aspects of racism, many whites began to defend their positions with claims of constitutional rights, including the right of freedom of association. But by the 1960s, new formulations began to appear in letters and public statements, in everyday locutions like "I am not racist, but . . ." or "I believe that everyone is the same, whether black, white, yellow, purple, or green." Whites are quick to deny, usually vehemently, accusations of racism, but more than that, just as quick to offer up evidence of their tolerance and open-mindedness. The very frequency of such professions of antiracism suggests the deep impact of political, religious, and educational efforts to delegitimate prejudice but, at the same time, nagging insecurity about the persistence of racial animosity.[31]

Above all, white Americans lived a paradox. How could they embody their antiracism—their color blindness—when in overwhelming numbers they continued to live in racially segregated communities and sent their children to racially segregated schools, and seldom interacted in a meaningful everyday way with people of different racial backgrounds?

As whites began to repudiate their racism publicly, they also grew increasingly optimistic about race relations in the United States. That optimism rested on both their own self-perceptions that they were no longer racist, and also on their interpretation of 1960s civil rights legislation. The abolition of de jure Jim Crow in public accommodations—the result of Title II of the 1964 Civil Rights Act—led almost overnight to the disappearance of the most egregious forms of racial apartheid. Separate black and white drinking fountains, commonplace in the South through the 1960s, were a thing of the past. And throughout the country, both publicly enforced and privately mandated Jim Crow waned quickly. Hotels and restaurants, which had regularly discriminated against blacks because of local ordinance in much of the South and because of deeply entrenched custom in most of the North, were now open to all paying customers regardless of the color of their skin; blacks were no longer confined to the back of the bus or the "crow's nest" in movie theaters. Although the disappearance of these obvious forms of segregation was a major victory, it was by no means the end of racial inequality. Yet most whites thought that it was. By the 1970s, most whites agreed that blacks were equal—by the 1980s and 1990s, a sizable minority of whites went even further and contended that blacks enjoyed advantages over whites in many arenas of life because of programs like affirmative action in hiring, college admissions, and government contracting.[32]

Further reinforcing the virtue of color blindness is the

emphasis on diversity and its result—the growing number of nonwhite faces in formerly white-dominated institutions. As sociologist Orlando Patterson has argued, "Today we find racial equality in its political, civic, and cultural forms at a level that far exceeds any other advanced society, or even any of the large plural societies of the developing world."[33] The dramatic shift in the composition of student bodies at elite institutions of higher education and in the ranks of white-collar workers in major corporations has created extraordinary opportunity for a relatively small cadre of highly credentialed minorities. But changes—changes in representation at the top—seldom trickle down. There is no necessary correlation between the diversification of the elite and the structures of racial equality in everyday life. The symbolic incorporation of minorities and discursive shifts about race have not profoundly altered patterns of residential segregation or urban poverty, though they have accomplished change on the margins. Diversity has proven to be an indirect route, at best, to racial equality—although it has played a crucial role in reinforcing the perception that the barriers to black advancement have all but disappeared.[34]

If the proposition that America is a color-blind society is widely accepted, it still has different valences. Perhaps most widespread is what I will call normative color blindness, namely, a call for the rejection of all color-based categories and a skepticism of any official recognition of racial difference, whether it be in statistics gathering, self-identification, or medical or scientific research. This version of race-neutrality first manifested itself in state- and local-level antidiscrimination ordinances in the post–World War II years, when lawmakers regularly forbade the use of racial classifications in job and housing advertisements, in employment offices, and in public accommodations. Normative color blindness shaped the language of the 1964 Civil Rights Act, and it has, in the post-1960s era, become a staple of national politics, across the political spectrum. Advocates of normative color blindness hold that racial categorization, however well-intentioned, reinforces or reifies a problematic, essentialist understanding of race. The best way to ensure opportunities for African Americans—in this view—is to stop talking about race.

If there is a broad consensus on color blindness as a principle, it takes different political forms. On the right, the most influential is laissez-faire color blindness. Conservative advocates of color blindness argue that the United States crossed a critical threshold with the civil rights legislation of the mid-1960s. Civil rights laws rendered unconstitutional the use of any racial classifications, no matter how ostensibly benign the purpose. A corollary to this argument holds that, as the result of the eradication of formal, state-sanctioned discrimination, any remaining racial inequality is residual, the result of individual behavioral or cultural deficiencies. In this view, government programs—not racism—exacerbate inequality. Black poverty is the result of social programs like welfare that create "perverse incentives" by promoting "dependency" rather than "self-sufficiency." Programs that target racial minorities, such as affirmative action in hiring, contracting, and university admissions, or provide special assistance to minority home buyers, instantiate a poisonous notion of racial difference in public policy. And most importantly, racial preferences are patently unfair to whites. Color-blind public policies should reward individuals on the basis of their own merit—the content of their character rather than the color of their skin. Such an approach leaves the fate of individuals to the discipline of the market.[35]

On the left are advocates of a strategic color blindness,

who might acknowledge the persistence of racial inequality, but who contend that attention focused on race-specific grievances generates political liabilities that outweigh any benefits. In this view, an emphasis on racial disparities stokes a backlash politics, inhibiting the formation of an interracial coalition necessary for the revitalization of social democratic policies that will mitigate inequality. Those activists, academics, and politicians who continue to insist on racial disparities and discrimination play to white guilt and, in the process, alienate those who are not culpable for past acts of discrimination. Those who call for strategic color blindness often push for "universal" policies that provide benefits to disadvantaged people regardless of their race or ethnicity, in lieu of "targeted" programs that specify racial or ethnic beneficiaries. Many call for class-based programs, such as affirmative action programs that benefit low-income people regardless of color, or pro-labor and social welfare policies that address the common plight of the working poor, across racial boundaries. Some advocates of strategic color blindness suggest that those programs will address racial injustice in the United States as a side benefit, but not as a stated goal.[36]

Barack Obama struggled with the question of color blindness, most explicitly in his 2005 political memoir, *The Audacity of Hope*. "Rightly or wrongly, white guilt has exhausted itself in America," wrote Obama. "[E]ven the most fair-minded of whites, those who would genuinely like to see racial inequality ended and poverty relieved, tend to push back against suggestions of racial victimization—or race-specific claims based on the history of race discrimination in this country." It was one of his more perceptive observations—and one that fundamentally shaped his political strategy in both the primaries and the general election. Keenly aware of white exhaustion, Obama stepped delicately around the still-persistent problems of racial inequality. Instead he offered an implicit promise, namely, that his election would embody color blindness, offering definitive proof that skin color no longer barred anyone's aspirations to success. Obama's success would mark, symbolically, the full incorporation of minorities into a diverse nation. In other words, Obama's race mattered as proof positive of America's race-neutrality.

Obama's opponents—equally aware of that white exhaustion—latched onto even the Obama campaign's slightest suggestions of race-based unfairness to make the claim that Obama was "playing the race card"—sometimes, as John McCain put it, "from the bottom of the deck," or, in its most extreme versions, that by mentioning race, Obama had become a "reverse racist," who held whites in contempt. To expand his base of support among whites and to dodge his opponents' criticism, Obama had every political incentive to avoid racially charged issues. His self-enforced silence on racial issues was evidence of his realpolitik, but more importantly a reminder of how the rhetoric of color blindness obscured the persistence of the color line and marginalized those who had the audacity to try to challenge it.[37]

But in March 2008, in the aftermath of a furor around a videotape of one of his pastor's sermons, Obama could dodge the issue no more. Although news accounts focused on snippets of Jeremiah Wright's rhetoric, the roaring incantation "God Damn America," repeated in endless loops, was enough to arouse Obama's critics and unsettle many of his supporters. Commentators asked hard questions. Was the "postracial" candidate really a crypto–black nationalist? Did he endorse what critics called the venomous "race hate"—the black "racism"—emanating from Wright's pulpit? Obama had no choice but to distance himself from Wright's most inflammatory words, though he did so subtly and sensitively.

Rather than going on the defensive, he turned what was a crisis of legitimacy into an extraordinary opportunity—and in the process offered a powerful, sophisticated, and wide-ranging address, surely the most learned disquisition on race from a major political figure ever.

Delivered at the National Constitution Center in Philadelphia, Obama's speech, "A More Perfect Union," was, like the best political speeches, as noteworthy for its elisions and its silences as for its content. It offered the fullest glimpse into Obama's framework for thinking about the paradox of race in our time. In a brilliant synthesis, he combined the personal, the historical, the normative, and the proscriptive. It was on one level his attempt to assuage concerns about his association with "black militancy" and distance himself from a grievance-based politics of race that alienated potential white support. But Obama did something much more significant. He offered Americans a way past the nation's deepest-rooted divisions by acknowledging the troubled past and its current legacy, and laying out the principles for a public policy that would provide a way out.

There are four major themes in his speech. First, Obama acknowledged ongoing racial divisions—although, notably, he mostly put them in the past tense. Second, he suggested the moral equivalence of black anger at discrimination and white backlash. Third, he celebrated hybridity and, building on the themes of his autobiography, branded himself as the embodiment of an alternative America where racial distinctions blur into something new. Fourth, he called for a "more perfect union" of black, white, and Latino, working-class and middle-class, bound together by a common national purpose. It was his endorsement of normative color blindness. Finally, turning toward public policy, he called for the creation of a multiracial governing coalition, spearheaded by working-class blacks, whites, and Latinos—a strategic color blindness—to address the still-persistent problems of economic injustice in American society. In its entirety, the speech was the synthesis of a synthesis, reiterating themes that had coursed through Obama's political rhetoric since his days as a grassroots organizer in Chicago, but packaging them into a whole as he never had before. In the paragraphs that follow, I focus on each of these themes in turn.

Racial division. Obama candidly acknowledges the burdens of history on the present, pointing to what he calls the "original sin of slavery," written into the Constitution itself. And he offers a long view of the efforts to overcome that sin through "protests and struggle, on the streets and in the courts, through a civil war and civil disobedience" that eventually narrowed "the gap between the promise of our ideals and the reality of their time." Obama moves forward to the twentieth century—bringing the history of that "sin" into the lifetimes of many of his listeners. "So many of the disparities that exist in the African American community today can be directly traced to inequalities passed on from the past." Drawing from specialized academic research on race and inequality in urban America, he links the Federal Housing Administration's discriminatory policies—policies that between 1934 and 1968 restricted government-backed mortgages to racially homogeneous neighborhoods—to the contemporary black-white wealth gap, demonstrating a sophisticated understanding of the ways that public policy structures inequality. And he acknowledges the long-term effects of the exclusion of blacks from unions and public employment. It is an extraordinary history lesson.

But here, Obama shifts tone very quickly. He falls back into the past tense, describing this world as the "reality in which Reverend Wright and other African Americans of his generation grew up. They came of age in the late fifties and early sixties. . . ." His core message—one that grows out of his view of civil rights history and Wilsonian sociology—is that of discontinuity. Discrimination, for Obama, is mostly history; grievances against racial inequality, like those in Reverend Wright's sermons, are rooted not in a candid assessment of the present, but rather in the experience of an older generation. "What's remarkable," states Obama, "is not how many failed in the face of discrimination, but rather how many men and women overcame the odds." The power of Obama's use of history comes from his recognition of a fundamental American optimism, one that Gunnar Myrdal recognized some six decades ago, when he wrote of the "boundless, idealistic aspirations" of "the American Creed."[38]

Equivalence. Obama highlights black anger—an anger that "may not get expressed in public, in front of white co-workers or white friends," but which "does find voice in the barbershop or around the kitchen table." Here Obama speaks from his own experience of organizing door-to-door in the Altgeld Gardens housing projects, sitting in the pews of Trinity United Church of Christ, or attending hundreds of community meetings and campaign events in his mostly black Illinois State Senate district. It is a line that also reflects the deep pessimism about race prevailing in the United States, even at the moment that Obama was vaulting onto the national stage. In the fall of 2007, just as Obama launched his campaign, survey researchers for the Pew Foundation reported that two-thirds of blacks believed that they "almost always" or "frequently" faced discrimination in the workplace and when renting or buying a house or apartment. And more than half of blacks reported discrimination in retail and restaurants. Obama validates their bitterness and deep skepticism about white America: "But the anger is real; it is powerful; and to simply wish it away, to condemn it without understanding its roots, only serves to widen the chasm of misunderstanding that exists between the races." This is perhaps the most powerful passage in the entire speech.[39]

Obama follows with what is surely the most problematic section of the speech—his discussion of white backlash. He accurately portrays the vulnerability and insecurity of working-class whites, echoing his efforts to win over working-class white voters on the campaign trail, especially in the aftermath of the Clinton campaign's charge that he was "out of touch," and news reports that his "elitism" alienated Joe Six-Pack. To emphasize his sympathy with blue-collar whites, he lists white racial grievances, invoking arguments popularized by journalists and pundits during the mid- and late 1980s that civil rights is a zero-sum game that exacts high costs from whites. Those who resent busing (an issue that has been off the table for the last several decades in most parts of the country), and who chafe at affirmative action in higher education and in the workplace, are, in Obama's telling, as justified in their outrage as are those blacks who continue to experience discrimination, even though there is little evidence that whites have been harmed by affirmative action or other compensatory programs. At a moment when many ordinary citizens—and most recently the Supreme Court, in its Seattle and Louisville school desegregation decisions—argue that white racism and black racism coexist as fundamental moral equivalents, Obama offers his own concurring opinion.[40]

Hybridity. A secondary but still significant theme in Obama's Philadelphia speech is the instability and fluidity of racial and ethnic categories in an America where immigration and interracial marriage, like that of his own parents, are challenging conventional notions of race and identity. Obama's speech captures—perhaps better than anything in print—the paradoxes of race in late twentieth-century America, at a moment when the nation's population is arguably more diverse than it has been since the great immigration wave of the late nineteenth and early twentieth centuries. It is something of a cliché to describe contemporary America as a "hyphen-nation," a place where identities are multiple, fragmented, and contested, but it is not one that Obama accepts. Reiterating a theme from his memoirs, Obama begins his Philadelphia speech by defining himself as fundamentally American, but at the same time as one who embodies the promise of a new postracial order. "I am the son of a black man from Kenya and a white woman from Kansas. I was raised with the help of a white grandfather who survived a Depression to serve in Patton's Army during World War II and a white grandmother who worked on a bomber assembly line at Fort Leavenworth while he was overseas. I've gone to some of the best schools in America and lived in one of the world's poorest nations. I am married to a black American who carries within her the blood of slaves and slave owners—an inheritance we pass on to our two precious daughters. I have brothers, sisters, nieces, nephews, uncles and cousins, of every race and every hue, scattered across three continents, and for as long as I live, I will never forget that in no other country on Earth is my story even possible."

The hybridity that Obama embodies is both cultural and aspirational: one that resonates deeply with the language of color blindness prevailing in modern America, and that highlights the indeterminacy of racial identities, the fluidity of self in late twentieth- and early twenty-first-century America. It is a powerful culmination of Obama's quest for racial identity that finally moves past Malcolm X, John Lewis, and even Martin Luther King, Jr. (and in a certain way returns home to the place that he scarcely mentioned on the campaign trail,

Hawaii). It also builds on a rhetoric of diversity that dates back to the intercultural education movement of the 1930s and 1940s—a movement that called for a celebration of the contributions of distinctive groups to American history— and reflects the argument that Supreme Court Justice Lewis Powell articulated in his concurring opinion in the landmark *Bakke* decision, that America is a "nation of many peoples." And it reinforces a view that racial assimilation is the core of American exceptionalism, a position belied by the experiences of racial and ethnic minorities in countries as diverse as Canada, France, and Sweden, which are far from utopian, but where interracial marriage is more common than it is in the United States, and where rates of residential segregation are much lower. Yet, Kansan or Kenyan, European or African American, Obama lives in an America where the principle of hypodescent—the one-drop rule—still shapes perceptions of those of African heritage, even if it scarcely corresponds to the polychromatic, multiethnic reality of the United States. For Obama, as for a growing number of Americans of European, Latin American, and Asian descent, hybridity is a choice. But for most Americans of African descent adopting a hybrid identity is nearly impossible—and for many, indeed, undesirable.[41]

Coalition. Obama's speech culminates in the call for a "more perfect union," a redolent phrase that conflates coalition politics and national mission, at once aspirational and pragmatic. Obama roots national identity in the commonality of wartime sacrifice, in the shared experience of "the men and women of every color and creed who serve together, and fight together, and bleed together under the same flag." It is evocative language that highlights the consanguinity of nationhood while challenging old associations of blood and race. Obama's call for a "more perfect union" evokes Lincolnian themes, but in service of pragmatic efforts to address pressing social and economic problems. For Obama "union" is both a means and an end. "I believe deeply that we cannot solve the challenges of our time unless we solve them together—unless we perfect our union by understanding that we may have different stories but common hopes; that we may not look the same and we may not have come from the same place but we all want to move in the same direction." But, ultimately, commonality is less the result of shared sacrifice or shared hopes than of shared grievances: "the crumbling schools that are stealing the future of black children and white children and Hispanic children . . . the hospitals that fail people of all backgrounds . . . the shuttered mills that once provided a decent life for men and women of every race and the homes for sale that once belonged to Americans from every religion, every region, every walk of life." Union is at once teleological, the outcome of a long, national process of perfectionism, and processual, the outcome of "talk" and the sharing of "different stories"; but ultimately it is coalitional, the minimization of difference in service of common national goals, specifically the election of Barack Obama and the enactment of public policies to improve education and health care, to restore industry and shore up homeownership.

≡

Obama's speech ultimately leaves many questions unanswered, especially in the everyday realm of policymaking. How can a recognition of difference and a call for unity translate into public policy? How will Obama deal with the persistence of racial inequality and with the legacies of public policies that created and reinforced racial discrimination? Obama's rhetoric suggests his attraction to "universal" rather than "targeted" social programs. But his acknowledgment of the persistence of discrimination and the legacy of slavery suggests his willingness to maintain and defend civil rights legislation that takes race into account to overcome racial inequalities. Tensions abound in Obama's emphasis at once on difference and on unity, on racial division and hybridity, on the fundamental equivalence of black and white racial grievances. What are the policy implications of Obama's vision of race?

Because racial issues have remained largely secondary—or even tertiary—in Obama's first year in office, overwhelmed by the international financial crisis, the debate about health insurance reform, the escalation of the war in Afghanistan and the ongoing military engagement in Iraq, any assessment will be, by necessity, incomplete. But his administration's initial efforts suggest a rhetorical and programmatic commitment that is consistent with the positions he took during his presidential campaign.

The first policy Obama suggests—a fusion of his Clintonian liberalism and Christian moralism—is a call for personal responsibility. It is one that he reiterates in the Philadelphia speech, echoing arguments voiced in his 2004 address to the Democratic National Convention, and in his speeches to black leaders and civil rights activists at Selma in 2007, at Ebenezer Baptist Church in Atlanta in 2008, and to the centenary convention of the NAACP in 2009. The NAACP speech, in particular, embodies Obama's hybrid approach: reflecting on discrimination as well as "structural inequalities that our nation's legacy of discrimination has left behind," asking support for Democratic education and health care programs, and, in the section of the speech that generated the most comment, reiterating his call for African Americans to adopt "a new mind set, a new set of attitudes" and to accept "our responsibility" for raising children to aspire to excellence. "I want them aspiring to be scientists and engineers—doctors and teachers—not just ballers and rappers."[42] In this respect, Obama is pursuing a time-honored presidential tradition—using the Oval Office as a bully pulpit. But, more than Clinton, whose calls for personal responsibility were divorced from his own personal lifestyle, the first African American president also hopes to serve as a role model for African Americans, even if there is little evidence that exhortation and personal example will have much of an impact on the underlying causes of poverty.

When it comes to whites, however, Obama has usually stepped down from his bully pulpit, dodging the political risks of highlighting personal or group responsibility and, instead, calling for greater dialogue and education. Unlike Obama's exhortations for black personal responsibility, which aroused suspicion only among a small number of analysts on the political left, his mere suggestion of white racism sparked a firestorm. During the Democratic primary in Pennsylvania, for example, Obama faced outrage for suggesting that his own grandmother was afraid of black men and "uttered racial or ethnic stereotypes that made me cringe," and then, in an interview, calling her a "typical white person." And, during the general election, Obama took heat for his humorous aside that he "doesn't look like all those other presidents on the dollar bills," leading campaign spokesman Robert Gibbs to disingenuously state that the remark was "not about race," before campaign adviser David Axelrod admitted that it was. Obama's political team learned a lesson from those flaps: act with restraint, even when confronted with overt racism. On the campaign trail and in office, Obama was besieged by racist hate mail and was caricatured variously as a "racist" with a "deep-seated hatred for white people or the white culture," an African witch doctor, a monkey, and a dangerous outsider because of his Kenyan descent. Bloggers reported extensively on racial denunciations of Obama, and some prominent commentators, among them former president Jimmy Carter, charged Obama's detractors as racist, but Obama steadfastly refused to chastise his race-baiting critics, treating them as distractions rather than real threats.[43]

As president, Obama was once again reminded of the high cost of frank talk about race, this time in the aftermath of the arrest of Harvard African American studies professor Henry Louis Gates, Jr., at his Cambridge, Massachusetts, house by a white police officer, James Crowley, after Gates and a taxi driver gained entry to the house by prying open a broken lock. The incident angered the usually unflappable Obama, because of both his friendship with Gates and his long-standing concern with police profiling. At the end of a lengthy press conference on health care in July 2009, Obama offered an unscripted response to a question about the Gates controversy, pointedly stating that the Cambridge police "acted stupidly in arresting somebody when there was already proof that they were in their own home." Obama went on to offer a brief history lesson, namely, that what "we know separate and apart from this incident is that there is a long history in this country of African-Americans and Latinos being stopped by law enforcement disproportionately. And that's just a fact." Obama's uncharacteristic candor backfired. Conservatives lambasted Obama as a "racist" and as antipolice, a position that was reiterated by many law enforcement officials, including Crowley and his superiors, who accused Obama of inappropriately interfering in a police matter and insulting the arresting officer without full knowledge of the facts of the case. Commentators and bloggers scrutinized the incident and Obama's reaction from nearly every angle. Two days after the press conference, Obama attempted to diffuse the situation, stating that "I could've calibrated those words differently," and inviting both Crowley and Gates to meet him over beers at the White House. It was a symbolic gesture, offering respect to both aggrieved parties, but ultimately backing down from what had become too hot to handle. The incident was a reminder both of the danger of discussing racial issues— even something as well-documented as police harassment of minority suspects—and of the limitation of the White House as bully pulpit. It was telling that Obama's exhortation to blacks to shape up was ultimately far less controversial than was his criticism of police misconduct.[44]

The presidency, however, has far greater powers than those of education and persuasion. Historically, the most significant civil rights advances have come not from exhortation, but instead from government using its authority—expanding civil rights legislation, broadening the scope of civil rights law through litigation, and, especially, using its regulatory and enforcement powers to undermine discrimination. Beginning in the mid-1960s, for example, federal enforcement of Title VII of the Civil Rights Act opened up significant job opportunities for African Americans and other minorities in workplaces once closed to them. Likewise, federal enforcement of the Voting Rights Act of 1965 played a major role in eliminating discriminatory electoral practices and expanding the number of black elected officials, especially in the South. By contrast, in the absence of strong enforcement power—as in the case of Title VIII of the Civil Rights Act, the 1968 law that forbade housing discrimination—patterns of racial segregation barely changed. The White House bully pulpit has never been sufficient, in its own right, to transform institutions. It has taken the coercive power of the law to make appreciable changes in African Americans' status in American society.[45]

That lesson was especially clear during the George W. Bush administration when the Department of Justice systematically withdrew resources from civil rights enforcement, marginalized many staff civil rights attorneys, and hired inexperienced but outspokenly conservative career attorneys in violation of civil service provisions. Altogether 236 career civil rights lawyers left the DOJ between 2003 and 2007 (out of a staff of about 350), many alienated by the increasingly politicized atmosphere there. In addition, Bush's Justice Department nearly ceased litigating housing and employment cases, shifted energy away from minority voting rights cases to allegations of voter fraud, and filed relatively few amicus briefs in support of privately litigated civil rights cases.[46]

As a civil rights attorney and a scholar of constitutional law, Obama well knew how effective the federal enforcement of civil rights laws could be in eliminating discrimination, and saw clearly the costs of inaction. In a speech at Howard University, shortly after announcing his campaign for the presidency, Obama unsparingly criticized "a Justice Department whose idea of prosecuting civil rights violations is trying to rollback affirmative action programs at our colleges and universities; a Justice Department whose idea of prosecuting voting rights violations is to look for voting fraud in black and Latino communities where it doesn't exist." At Howard, and in his campaign platform, Obama pledged that he would staff the Civil Rights Division "with civil rights lawyers who prosecute civil rights violations, and employment discrimination, and hate crimes. And we'll have a Voting Rights Section that actually defends the right of every American to vote without deception or intimidation." As president, Obama quietly but aggressively upheld his promise. Under his attorney general, Eric Holder, the Department of Justice began stepping up civil rights enforcement (though its efforts were hindered by Republican senators who used Senate rules to put a hold on the confirmation hearings for his nominee for deputy attorney general for civil rights). Even without Obama's nominee at the head of the Civil Rights Division, the DOJ turned its attention to "high impact" discrimination cases. It filed briefs supporting affirmative action in the New Haven firefighters case (struck down by the Supreme Court), argued on behalf of maintaining preclearance provisions in voting rights enforcement (the requirement that districts with a history of discrimination get Department of Justice approval for changes in voting arrangements), and supported a lawsuit (won in a federal court in New York) that requires Westchester County, New York, communities to construct affordable housing to expand options for minorities in the job-rich suburbs. Although centrists hoped that Obama would find a "third way" between "liberal racialists who believe that we've made little progress on race since the 1960s," and conservatives who "insist that anti-discrimination laws are no longer necessary," Obama's DOJ has resisted narrowing civil rights law from a focus on disparate impact to discriminatory intent, and has called for the strict enforcement of existing laws.[47]

Obama has made it clear that antidiscrimination law is only one part of his effort to deal with racial inequality—and not the most crucial. Of critical importance, especially in the midst of the Great Recession, is unemployment and underemployment, but the administration's efforts to alleviate unemployment took a backseat to its program to bail out troubled financial institutions. As a result, while the stock market rebounded and leading investment banks posted profits, joblessness rose. By November 2009, unemployment rates in the United States had gone into the double digits. African Americans and Latinos disproportionately bore the burden of joblessness: almost 16 percent of blacks and 13 percent of Latinos, compared to 9.5 percent of whites, were out of work. Young blacks were the worst affected by the downturn: 30.5 percent of blacks between the ages of eighteen and twenty-four were unemployed nationwide. The job creation component of Obama's stimulus package, which, if William Julius Wilson was right should disproportionately benefit minorities, met with mixed results at best. The stimulus put a priority on "shovel ready" construction projects—aiding a sector of the economy dominated by men and, despite decades of civil rights activism and affirmative action efforts, still disproportionately white. In the hardest-hit cities, the impact of federal job spending was scarcely visible. Just a year after Obama was elected, a coalition of civil rights and labor groups, led by the venerable National Association for the Advancement of Colored People and the National Council of La Raza, demanded that his administration step up its job creation efforts. "Make no mistake, for us this is the civil rights issue of the moment," argued civil rights leader Wade Henderson. "Unless we resolve the national job crisis, it will make it hard to address all of our other priorities."[48]

While the administration has not put a priority on job creation, one of its signature programs—health care reform—could have an important labor market impact, especially for African Americans (and increasingly Latinos), who have benefited from the dramatic expansion of health-related employment in the period since the 1960s. Increased funding for scientific and medical research will benefit urban teaching hospitals, which provide a wide range of jobs for minority workers and professionals, from janitors to clerks, from orderlies and aides to nurses and doctors. Even more importantly, health insurance reform promises to have a stimulative effect on employment in the medical sector, particularly in the big city hospitals that have traditionally served uninsured patients.[49]

Of all of the causes of racial inequality, the one that has

most animated Obama has been education. In his Philadelphia speech, Obama forcefully reiterated a now-unpopular argument for racial integration in public education. "Segregated schools were, and are, inferior schools; we still haven't fixed them, fifty years after *Brown v. Board of Education*, and the inferior education they provided, then and now, helps explain the pervasive achievement gap between today's black and white students." But Obama's educational policies in practice de-emphasize integration. Regarding schooling, Obama has echoed his antipoverty message, offering the bromides of "self-discipline" and "hard work."[50]

But despite his rhetorical nod to *Brown*, Obama's educational policy takes for granted the persistence of racially segregated schools, despite evidence that racial and socioeconomic diversity in schools is strongly correlated with better educational outcomes. Pro-integrative policies are politically unpopular: many African Americans have accepted racial segregation, so long as their schools are funded at a level comparable to that of majority-white schools. And most whites accept school segregation as a natural consequence of market choices, while remaining indifferent at best, actively opposed at worst, to even voluntary programs to desegregate schools. The consequence is that at the same time that the Obama administration has expanded federal funding for public education, it has neither mandated nor provided incentives for school desegregation. The American Recovery and Reinvestment Act (the Obama administration's stimulus package) set aside a $650 million Innovation Fund for schools that closed achievement gaps. But to that end, the Department of Education has called for the expansion of charter schools and has advocated for such programs as the Harlem Children's Zone, which provides preschool and enrichment programs for students in disadvantaged neighborhoods. Whether either model is effective is unclear. Thus far, data show that educational improvements in charter schools are no better than marginal. Programs like Harlem's Children Zone have demonstrated real gains at the preschool level, but have proven far less effective for middle and high school students. And both initiatives reinforce patterns of educational segregation, rather than providing resources to pro-integrative programs that demonstrably improve educational outcomes.[51]

Educational inequality and housing inequality have long been intertwined because of educational localism in the United States. Wealthy communities have long benefited from well-funded schools; poorer and racially segregated communities have been burdened with second-class education. The Obama administration's urban and metropolitan initiatives—especially its programs to mitigate the impact of predatory lending, to expand the construction of affordable housing, and to open long-segregated suburban housing markets—have been limited so far, but have the potential to address structural inequalities head-on. For the first time since the 1970s, when Jimmy Carter created a short-lived and ultimately ill-fated Urban Policy Research Group, the White House has put cities and their metropolitan regions at the center of the national agenda, most prominently by creating a White House Office of Urban Affairs. Obama's pledge to create a comprehensive urban policy promises to reverse the course of the last three decades, during which cities and their poorest residents have been pretty close to the bottom of the list of presidential priorities. The first Bush administration introduced place-based investment policies through its Enterprise Zone program (renamed and slightly modified as Empowerment Zones by Clinton). But neither program was well funded; both had negligible effects in stemming urban disinvestment. The Obama administration's stimulus package funding, by contrast, has targeted urban and metropolitan areas for infrastructure projects. And some of the administration's assistance to foreclosed homeowners will benefit urban residents—although minority neighborhoods in urban centers are still reeling from the effects of a generation of predatory lending and high-interest mortgages.[52]

And the Obama administration has promised—but not yet moved very far—to improve on previous administrations' urban policies. Even the most innovative programs, like Hope VI, have been enacted in a rather piecemeal fashion. Federal efforts to replace public housing with market-rate and mixed-income public-private developments—an especially important policy since the Clinton years—have often displaced low-income housing residents without meeting the enormous demand for affordable housing, especially in expensive metropolitan areas. Unraveling this mess will not be easy. It requires interventions in housing policy, namely, far more aggressive programs than we have seen to date to open up metropolitan housing markets by race and class. It requires collaboration, including revenue sharing, across municipal boundaries. It requires breaching the very high governmental barriers that separate municipalities from each other. Regionalism is not a short-term solution to the problem of spatial inequity—but it is a necessary first step. Obama's rhetoric of unbounded community—his call to think outside the boundaries of narrow identity politics and self-interest—offers a challenge to some of the most poisonous manifestations of our bounded communities. In both policy and rhetoric, the new administration can challenge the "us versus them"/"city versus suburbs" ethos that reinforces racial, educational, and economic inequality in the United States.

≡

Whatever the impact of Obama's antipoverty, civil rights, education, and housing initiatives will be, it is clear that they are far from the top of his agenda. Those who expect that the first African American president will risk the political controversy of pushing hard on issues of racial equality might do well to listen to his own words. In the closing cadences of his mostly overlooked speech at Howard University's 2007 convocation, Obama offered one of his most astute readings of the history of race and social change in American history. It is a reminder of the fallacy of vesting hope for change in a single presidency; a harking back to his own distant past as a community organizer:

> But the truth is, one man cannot make a movement. No single law can erase the prejudice in the heart of a child who hangs a noose on a tree; or the callousness of a prosecutor who bypasses justice in the pursuit of vengeance. No one leader, no matter how shrewd or experienced, can prevent teenagers from killing other teenagers on the streets of our cities; or free our neighborhoods from the grip of hopelessness; or make real the promise of opportunity and equality for every citizen.

The path from past to future is seldom linear. The gains of Emancipation and Reconstruction gave way to the reenslavement of many African Americans. The near extinction of Native Americans one hundred years ago has been undone by the extraordinary increase in the number of Americans in the last third of a century who claim Amerindian descent. And the political resonance of ethnicity has waxed and waned from the nativist fears of the early twentieth century to the universalism of the New Deal to the revival of ethnicity in the 1970s to the polarized debate on immigration and citizenship today. What seem to be dramatic gains are often ephemeral, and what seem to be modest, incremental changes often, over time, prove to be momentous. With that history in mind, the impact of the election of Barack Obama as the forty-fourth president of the United States is unpredictable. And the future of race and inequality in the United States is not at all clear.

What is clear, however, is that whenever the arc of history has bent toward justice, this development has been the consequence of a synergy between grassroots activism and political leadership. The history of civil rights makes this lesson clear: the Franklin Delano Roosevelt administration made its first decisive move toward enforcing antidiscrimination in the defense industry (the Fair Employment Practices Committee) because the March on Washington Movement forced him to do so. Civil rights activists perceived the Kennedy administration as pliable to its demands, despite John F. Kennedy's indifferent record on civil rights and his reluctance to alienate his party's powerful Southern wing. Systematic pressure—culminating in the nationwide wave of demonstrations and disruption in the summer of 1963—pushed Kennedy to begin the drafting of civil rights legislation. It mattered that both those administrations were open to pressure. And it mattered that grassroots activists and civil rights organizations worked with the White House and put pressure on it from the outside.

Obama represents the paradox of race in early twenty-first-century America: he embodies the fluidity and opportunity of racial identity in a time of transition. He also captures the ambiguities of a racial order that denies racism yet is rife with racial inequality; that celebrates progress when celebration is not always warranted. He contains within his own thought contradictory positions that remain in tension with each other. And he brings to the table an openness to grapple with the still-unresolved history of race and rights, and the constraints of an elected official averse to controversy. His awareness of history and its burdens provides the rest of us with a challenge and an opportunity. Ultimately, whether the United States witnesses a post-Obama period of racial progress, or stasis, or regression depends to an extent on his policies. But those policies depend on us.

Acknowledgments

≡

I am greatly indebted to Dan Rodgers, director of the Shelby Cullom Davis Center for Historical Studies at Princeton, and Brigitta van Rheinberg, editor in chief of Princeton University Press, for inviting me to deliver the 2009 Lawrence Stone Lectures in History. My audience at Princeton was especially lively. I'd like to single out Tom Bender, Dirk Hartog, Tera Hunter, and Julian Zelizer for their intelligent questions and comments. I haven't yet met Paul Harvey to thank him in person, but his thoughtful review of my book *Sweet Land of Liberty*, published in *Books and Culture* during election week in November 2008, got me thinking about writing this one. I bounced ideas about Obama's relationship to the black freedom struggle off the graduate students in my spring 2009 seminar on the history of civil rights, and they bounced even more back. Props to Adam Goodman, Che Gossett, Rachel Guberman, Julia Gunn, Danielle Holtz, Erika Kitzmiller, Linda Maldonado, Peter Pihos, Sarah Rodriguez, and Jeffrey Silver. I am lucky to have lots of great conversationalists in my life, including several friends, colleagues, and students who might not even have known that they were serving as sounding boards for my ideas, but who helped me immensely, including Merlin Chowkwanyun, Andrew Diamond, Greg Goldman, Sally Gordon, Brittany Griebling, Steve Hahn,

Clem Harris, Liz Hersh, David Hollinger, Kevin Kruse, Lisa Levenstein, Pap Ndiaye, N. R. Popkin, Julia Rabig, Caroline Rolland-Diamond, Paul Schor, Bryant Simon, Peter Siskind, Jason Sokol, Heather Thompson, and Jean-Christian Vinel. Dan Amsterdam led a flock of scurrying friends in helping me find a title. Gary Gerstle, Michael Katz, and two anonymous referees for Princeton read whole drafts and gave me valuable comments. Lauren Lepow provided expert copyediting. My wife, Dana Barron, and my children, Anna and Jack, tolerated my insane travel schedule and still gave me the time and support to write, and the love to keep me going.

I dedicate this book to Michael B. Katz, whose commitment to rigorous, engaged scholarship has long inspired my work. I treasure his friendship.

—Mount Airy, Philadelphia, December 2009

Notes

≡

Introduction

1. David A Hollinger, "Obama, the Instability of Color Lines, and the Promise of a Postethnic Future," *Callaloo* 31 (2008): 1033–37; for a nuanced discussion of Obama and racism, see John L. Jackson, Jr., "The Rising Stakes of Obamaphobia," *Chronicle of Higher Education*, online edition, August 13, 2009, http://chronicle.com/blogPost/The-Rising-Stakes-of/7668/; Eduardo Bonilla-Silva, "Are the Americas 'Sick with Racism' or Is It a Problem at the Poles?" *Ethnic and Racial Studies* 32 (2009): 1071–82; see, generally, "The Social Significance of Barack Obama: An Online Exchange," American Sociological Association, ContextsBlog, http://contexts.org/obama/.

2. Richard Thompson Ford, *The Race Card: How Bluffing about Bias Makes Race Relations Worse* (New York: Farrar, Straus, and Giroux, 2008).

Chapter I
"This Is My Story": Obama, Civil Rights, and Memory

1. The poem's origins are unknown. It was popularized by a National Public Radio broadcast on October 28, 2008, and attributed to Ed Welch, a job trainer in St. Louis. In a Google search, March 13, 2009, the poem appeared 46,700 times.

2. Henry Louis Gates, Jr., introduction to Steven J. Niven, *Barack Obama: A Pocket Biography of Our 44th President* (New York: Oxford University Press, 2009), 2, 3.

3. Gallup Poll, "Americans See Obama Election as Race Relations

Milestone," www.gallup.com/poll/111817/
Americans-See-Obama-Election-Race-Relations-Milestone-aspx.

4. *Time*, November 17, 2008, 13.

5. "Black and White, North and South," *New York Observer*, November 26, 2009.

6. Quotation: "Terre de la discrimination et de la relégation, les Etats-Unis ont fait un grand pas vers la redemption": Laurent Joffrin, "Yes, He Can," *Libération*, November 6, 2008. See also Pap Ndiaye, "A quand un Obama français?" *L'Express*, November 5, 2008; "'Égalite reelle': Le manifeste 'oui nous pouvons' soutenu par Bruni-Sarkozy," *Le Nouvel Observateur*, November 12, 2008; "European Press Review: Welcome Barack Obama," *Deutsche Welle*, November 5, 2009. I explore these issues in the Franco-American context in Thomas J. Sugrue, "Putting the Torch to Colorblindness: Race, Riots, and the Limits of Universalism in France and the United States" (paper presented at Université Charles-de-Gaulle–Lille III, June 19, 2009).

7. Barack Obama, "Selma Voting Rights March Commemoration," Selma, Alabama, March 4, 2007, http://www.barackobama .com/2007/03/04/selma_voting_rights_march_comm.php.

8. For variations on this theme, see Matt Bai, "Is Obama the End of Black Politics?" *New York Times Magazine,* August 10, 2009; David Remnick, "The Joshua Generation: Race and the Campaign of Barack Obama," *New Yorker*, November 17, 2008; Gwen Ifill, *The Breakthrough: Politics and Race in the Age of Obama* (New York: Doubleday, 2009).

9. David Farber and Beth Bailey, *The First Strange Place: Race and Sex in World War II Hawaii* (New York: Free Press, 1992), is an indispensable account of Hawaii's place in the modern American imagination.

10. For Obama's description of Hawaii, see Barack Obama, *Dreams from My Father: A Story of Race and Inheritance* (New York: Times Books, 1995), 23–25.

11. On multiculturalism in the 1970s, see, among others, Jonathan Zimmerman, *Whose America? Culture Wars in the Public Schools* (Cambridge, Mass.: Harvard University Press, 2002), 107–30; John David Skrentny, *The Minority Rights Revolution* (Cambridge, Mass.: Harvard University Press, 2002); and Matthew Frye Jacobson, *Roots Too: White Ethnic Revival in Post–Civil Rights America* (Cambridge, Mass.: Harvard University Press, 2006).

12. Obama, *Dreams from My Father*; see also Barack Obama, *The Audacity of Hope* (New York: Vintage Books, 2008), 36–37: David Mendell, *Obama from Promise to Power* (New York: Harper, 2008), 34; "Son Finds Inspiration in the Dreams of His Father," *Hyde Park Herald*, August 23, 1995.

13. Mendell, *Obama*, 36; Frances Fitzgerald, *America Revised: History Schoolbooks in the Twentieth Century* (New York: Random House, 1980); Joseph A. Rodriguez and Vicki Ruiz, "At Loose Ends: Twentieth-Century Latinos in Current United States History Textbooks," *Journal of American History* 86 (2000): 1689–99.

14. Stu Glauberman and Jerry Burns, *The Dream Begins: How Hawai'i Shaped Barack Obama* (Honolulu: Watermark Publishing, 2009).

15. Obama, *Dreams from My Father*, 85–86. W.E.B. Du Bois, *The Souls of Black Folks: Essays and Sketches* (Chicago: A. C. McClurg and Co., 1903), 3. For an excellent overview of the multivalent readings of Malcolm X, see Joe Wood, ed., *Malcolm X: In Our Own Image* (New York: St. Martin's Press, 1992).

16. Obama, *Dreams from My Father*, 76–77, 89–91, 139–40; on Davis, see Glauberman and Burns, *Dream Begins*, 110–24; and Kathryn Waddell Takara, "Frank Marshall Davis: Black Labor Activist and Outsider Journalist: Social Movements in Hawai'i," http://www2.hawaii.edu/~takara/frank_marshall_davis.htm; the most useful survey of black radicalism and black power to date is Peniel Joseph, *Waiting 'til the Midnight Hour: A Narrative History of Black Power* (New York: Henry Holt, 2007).

17. Obama, *Dreams from My Father*, 120–22, 139–40. He misidentifies Ture as "Touré." "Obama's Account of New York Years Often Differs from What Others Say," *New York Times*, October 30, 2007.

18. Ryan Lizza, "The Agitator: Barack Obama's Unlikely Political Education," *New Republic*, March 19, 2007.

19. Chana Kai Lee, *For Freedom's Sake: The Life of Fannie Lou Hamer* (Urbana: University of Illinois Press, 1999); John Lewis with Michael D'Orso, *Walking with the Wind: A Memoir of the Civil Rights Movement* (New York: Simon and Schuster, 1998); Thomas J. Sugrue, *Sweet Land of Liberty: The Forgotten Struggle for Civil Rights in the North* (New York: Random House, 2008), 306, 313–14.

20. Charles Payne, *I've Got the Light of Freedom: The Organizing*

Tradition and the Mississippi Freedom Struggle (Berkeley and Los Angeles: University of California Press, 1995); Barbara Ransby, *Ella Baker and the Black Freedom Movement: A Radical Democratic Vision* (Chapel Hill: University of North Carolina Press, 2002); Eric Burner, *And Gently He Shall Lead Them: Robert Parris Moses and Civil Rights in Mississippi* (New York: New York University Press, 1994).

21. Barack Obama, "Problems and Promise in the Inner City," *Illinois Issues* (1988), reprinted in *After Alinsky* (Springfield: Illinois State University, 1990). Available at http://illinoisissues.uis.edu/archives/2008/09/whyorg.html. This is an argument that many scholars of civil rights, myself among them, have made in recent years. See Sugrue, *Sweet Land of Liberty*.

22. William E. Nelson, Jr., and Philip J. Meranto, *Electing Black Mayors: Political Action in the Black Community* (Columbus: Ohio State University Press, 1977); David R. Colburn and Jeffrey S. Adler, eds., *African American Mayors: Race, Politics, and the American City* (Urbana: University of Illinois Press, 2001).

23. Jason Sokol, "The Color of American Political History" (paper delivered to the Penn Humanities Forum, March 2009). On Massachusetts's racial politics generally, see Jeanne Theoharis, "'We Saved the City': Black Struggles against Educational Inequality in Boston, 1960–76," *Radical History Review* 81 (2001): 61–93; Ronald Formisano, *Boston against Busing: Race, Class and Ethnicity in the 1960s and 1970s* (Chapel Hill: University of North Carolina Press, 1990); J. Anthony Lukas, *Common Ground: A Turbulent Decade in the Lives of Three American Families* (New York: Knopf, 1986); James Green, "In Search of Common Ground," *Radical America* 20, no. 5 (1987): 40–60; Sugrue, *Sweet Land of Liberty*, 386–88, 487–89.

24. Jeffrey Adler, "Introduction," in Colburn and Adler, *African American Mayors*, 1; Heather R. Parker, "Tom Bradley and the Politics of Race," in Colburn and Adler, *African American Mayors*, 153–77; Raphael Sonenschein, *Politics in Black and White: Race and Power in Los Angeles* (Princeton: Princeton University Press, 1993); John Bauman, "W. Wilson Goode: The Black Mayor as Urban Entrepreneur," *Journal of Negro History* 77 (1992): 141–58; Mary Summers and Philip A. Klinkner, "The Daniels Election in New Haven and the Failure of the Deracialization Hypothesis," *Urban Affairs Quarterly* 27 (1991): 202–15.

25. Ruth Ann Strickland and Marcia Lynn Whicker, "Comparing the Wilder and Gantt Campaigns: A Model for Black Candidate Success in Statewide Elections," *PS: Political Science and Politics* 25, no. 2 (June 1992): 204–12; Michael C. Dawson, *Behind the Mule: Race and Class in African American Politics* (Princeton: Princeton University Press, 1995), 184.

26. James Q. Wilson, *Negro Politics: The Search for Leadership* (Glencoe, Ill.: Free Press, 1960), 230–50. Arnold R. Hirsch, "The Cook County Democratic Machine and the Dilemma of Race, 1931–1987," in Richard M. Bernard, ed., *Snowbelt Cities: Metropolitan Politics in the Northeast and Midwest since World War II* (Bloomington: Indiana University Press, 1987), 63–90; William J. Grimshaw, *Bitter Fruit: Black Politics and the Chicago Machine, 1931–1991* (Chicago: University of Chicago Press, 1992); and, more generally, James R. Grossman, *Land of Hope: Chicago, Black Southerners and the Great Migration* (Chicago: University of Chicago Press, 1989), and Nicholas Lemann, *The Promised Land: The Great Migration and How It Changed America* (New York: Knopf, 1991).

27. For varying interpretations of Washington's election and career, see Paul Kleppner, *Chicago Divided: The Making of a Black Mayor* (DeKalb: Northern Illinois University Press, 1985); Gary Rivlin, *Fire on the Prairie: Chicago's Harold Washington and the Politics of Race* (New York: Henry Holt and Company, 1992); Arnold R. Hirsch, "Harold and Dutch: A Comparative Look at the First Black Mayors of Chicago and New Orleans," in Raymond A. Mohl, ed., *The Making of Urban America* (Wilmington, Del.: Scholarly Resources, 1997), 265–82; Melvin Holli and Paul M. Green, eds., *The Making of the Mayor, 1983 (Grand Rapids, Mich.: Eerdmans, 1984).*

28. Obama, *Dreams from My Father*, 146–48.

29. For statistics on black employment under Washington, see Patrick Joyce, "A Reversal of Fortunes: Black Empowerment, Political Machines, and City Jobs in New York and Chicago," *Urban Affairs Review* 32 (1997): 291–318; see also Barbara Ferman, *Challenging the Growth Machine: Neighborhood Politics in Chicago and Pittsburgh* (Lawrence: University Press of Kansas, 1996), 113–18.

30. Hirsch, "Harold and Dutch," 276.

31. Adolph Reed, *The Jesse Jackson Phenomenon* (New Haven: Yale University Press, 1986); Marshall Frady, *Jesse: The Life and Pilgrimage of Jesse Jackson* (New York: Random House, 1996).

32. "Jackson, Fans Reflect on Legacy of '84, '88 Bids," *Chicago Tribune*, June 27, 2004. I have removed editorial brackets.

33. Obama, "Problems and Promise in the Inner City"; Ferman, *Challenging the Growth Machine*, 111–23; Larry Bennett, "Postwar Redevelopment in Chicago: The Declining Politics of Party and the Rise of Neighborhood Politics," in Gregory D. Squires, ed., *Unequal Partnerships: The Political Economy of Urban Redevelopment in Postwar America* (New Brunswick, N.J.: Rutgers University Press, 1989), 171–75.

34. Flamboyant black urban politicians garnered extensive media attention, especially in the 1980s and the first half of the 1990s. For examples, see Jim Sleeper, *The Closest of Strangers: Liberalism and the Politics of Race in New York* (New York: W. W. Norton, 1990); Tamar Jacoby, *Someone Else's House: America's Unfinished Struggle for Integration* (New York: Random House, 2000).

35. William Tucker, "The Mystery of Wappingers Falls," *New Republic*, March 21, 1988, 19–22; Andrew Sullivan, "The Two Faces of Bensonhurst," *New Republic*, July 2, 1990, 13–16; Jim Sleeper, "New York Stories," *New Republic*, September 10, 1990, 20–22; Jonathan Reider, *Canarsie: The Jews and Italians of Brooklyn against Liberalism* (Cambridge, Mass.: Harvard University Press, 1985); Lukas, *Common Ground*; Sleeper, *The Closest of Strangers*; Thomas Byrne Edsall and Mary D. Edsall, *Chain Reaction: The Impact of Race, Rights, and Taxes on American Politics* (New York: W. W. Norton, 1991).

36. Among the most influential accounts of race, liberal politics, and the "culture wars," most of which began as journalistic or political projects in the 1980s and 1990s, is Todd Gitlin, *The Twilight of Common Dreams: Why America Is Wracked by Culture Wars* (New York: Metropolitan Books, 1995).

37. The Thernstrom case was popularized by Dinesh D'Souza, *Illiberal Education: The Politics of Race and Sex* (New York: Simon and Schuster, 1991); the fairest and most thorough account is Jon Wiener, *Historians in Trouble: Plagiarism, Fraud, and Politics in the Ivory Tower* (New York: The New Press, 2005), 58–70; Stephan Thernstrom, "McCarthyism Then and Now," *Academic Questions* 4, no. 1 (1990): 14–16.

38. Matthew S. Bromberg, "Harvard Law School's War over Faculty Diversity," *Journal of Blacks in Higher Education* 1 (Autumn 1993): 75–82, offers a useful summary of events there. The phrase "Beirut of

legal education," was coined by David Trubek, a critical legal theory scholar who was denied tenure in 1987, a little more than a year before Obama arrived. See "Harvard Tenure Battle Puts Critical Legal Studies on Trial," *New York Times*, August 30, 1987. For the sake of full disclosure, I note that I was a student at Harvard at the time, was a teaching assistant in Stephan Thernstrom's controversial course, and knew many law students, including several members of the *Harvard Law Review* and the Federalist Society, though to the best of my recollection I did not meet Obama at the time.

39. "First Black Elected to Head Harvard Law Review," *New York Times*, February 6, 1990; "Barack Obama's Law Personality," *Los Angeles Times*, March 19, 1990; "In Law School, Obama Found Political Voice," *New York Times*, January 28, 2007; "At Harvard Law, a Unifying Voice," *Boston Globe*, January 28, 2007; "Review President Explains Affirmative Action Policy," *Harvard Law Record*, November 16, 1990, reprinted in "Record Retrospective: Obama on Affirmative Action," *Harvard Law Record*, October 30, 2008.

40. Obama, *Dreams from My Father*, 134.

41. Mendell, *Obama*, 73; Taylor Branch, *Parting the Waters: America in the King Years, 1954–63* (New York: Simon and Schuster, 1988).

42. "New African-American Leaders Are Emerging," *Chicago Sun-Times*, September 1, 1999; "Race Shifts Seen in Remap Efforts—Leaders Struggle to Retain Wards," *Chicago Tribune*, October 14, 2001. There was a robust debate about minority voting rights in the late 1980s and 1990s. Key books from the period include Abigail Thernstrom, *Whose Votes Count? Affirmative Action and Minority Voting Rights* (Cambridge, Mass.: Harvard University Press, 1987), and Bernard Grofman and Chandler Davison, eds., *Controversies in Minority Voting: The Voting Rights Act in Perspective* (Washington, D.C.: The Brookings Institution, 1992).

43. Obama, *Dreams from My Father*, 139–40, 200, 203.

44. "Hyde Parker Announces Run for State Senate Seat," *Hyde Park Herald*, October 4, 1995; "Petition Challenges Shape Political Ballot," *Hyde Park Herald*, January 10, 1996; political scientist Adolph Reed, Jr., a Palmer supporter and longtime Obama critic, denounced the effort to disqualify Palmer as "vicious and under-handed." See "Local Independent Voters Still Divided," *Hyde Park Herald*, January 31, 1996.

45. Barack Obama, "Getting the Lead Out of Our Children," *Hyde Park Herald*, March 25, 1998; Barack Obama, "Education Most Important Town Hall Issue," *Hyde Park Herald*, April 29, 1998; "State Taxes Block Road off Welfare," *Chicago Tribune*, April 10, 1999; "'Racial Profiling' Target of Bill," *Chicago Tribune*, December 7, 1999; "New Law Extends Life of Economic Enterprise Zones," *Chicago Tribune*, January 12, 2001; "City, State Remap Bickering Dominates Year," *Hyde Park Herald*, December 26, 2001; "Obama Begins Raising Funds for U.S. Senate Bid," *Hyde Park Herald*, July 10, 2002; "Fight Racial Profiling at Local Level, Lawmaker Says," *Chicago Tribune*, June 29, 2003; "Big Dollars Boost Obama's Chances as Primary Looms," *Hyde Park Herald*, February 18, 2004.

46. Rush is worth a full biography. For background on the Chicago Panthers, see Jon Rice, "The World of the Illinois Panthers," in Jeanne Theoharis and Komozi Woodard, *Freedom North* (New York: Palgrave, 2003); for an overview of his congressional career, see "Is Bobby Rush in Trouble?" *Chicago Reader*, March 2000. "Soul Survivor: Bobby Rush," *Chicago Tribune*, November 16, 2003; Mendell, *Obama*, 128–39, offers the best account of the Rush-Obama congressional race in 2000.

47. There is a large body of scholarship on these issues. Some of the best works include Clarence Stone, *The Politics of Urban Development* (Lawrence: University Press of Kansas, 1987); Richard Keiser, *Subordination or Empowerment? African American Leadership and the Struggle for Urban Political Power* (New York: Oxford University Press, 1997); Adolph Reed, Jr., *Stirrings in the Jug: Black Politics in the Post Segregation Era* (Minneapolis: University of Minnesota Press, 1999), esp. chaps. 3–5.

48. "Rich 90s Failed to Lift All: Income Disparity between Races Widened Greatly, Census Analysis Shows," *Chicago Tribune*, August 20, 2002; Larry Bennett, Janet L. Smith, and Patricia A. Wright, eds., *Where Are Poor People to Live? Transforming Public Housing Communities* (Armonk, N.Y.: M. E. Sharpe, 2006); Paul Louis Street, *Racial Oppression in the Global Metropolis: A Living Black Chicago History* (Lanham, Md.: Rowman and Littlefield, 2007).

49. "Poor Live Housing Nightmare While Investors Reap Benefits—$150 Million from U.S. Fails to Fix Lawndale Apartments," *Chicago Tribune*, November 21, 2004; "Rezko Owns Vacant Lot Next to

Obama's Home," *Chicago Tribune*, November 1, 2006; "Soft-Spoken, Low-Key Casino Magnate—The Developer Has Been Called 'Chicago's Answer to Trump,'" *Philadelphia Inquirer*, October 27, 2006.

50. "Barack and Michelle Obama Begin Their Storied Journey," *Savoy*, February 2005, 60.

51. Quoted in Richard Wolffe and Darren Briscoe, "Across the Divide: Barack Obama's Road to Racial Reconstruction," *Newsweek*, July 16, 2007, 22–23.

52. Barack Obama, "A More Perfect Union" (speech delivered at the National Constitution Center, Philadelphia, March 18, 2008), http://my.barackobama.com/page/content/hisownwords.

53. In 2008, King ranked at the top of a roster of "American heroes" identified by high school students. See Sam Wineburg and Chauncey Monte-Sano, "'Famous Americans': The Changing Pantheon of American Heroes," *Journal of American History* 94 (2008): 1186–1202.

54. Thomas F. Jackson, *From Civil Rights to Human Rights: Martin Luther King, Jr., and the Struggle for Economic Justice* (Philadelphia: University of Pennsylvania Press, 2008); Michael Eric Dyson, *I May Not Get There with You: The True Martin Luther King, Jr.* (New York: Free Press, 2001); Michael Honey, *Going Down Jericho Road: The Memphis Strike, Martin Luther King Jr.'s Last Campaign* (New York: W. W. Norton, 2007).

55. For Wright's interpretation of King—which emphasized MLK's opposition to the Vietnam War, his criticism of capitalism, and his labor politics—see Jeremiah A. Wright, Jr., "Another Year, Another Chance," *Philadelphia Tribune*, January 7, 2007, and "Facing the Rising Sun," *Philadelphia Tribune*, April 22, 2007.

56. On these topics, my thinking has been shaped by Rogers Smith, *Civic Ideals: Conflicting Visions of Citizenship in U.S. History* (New Haven: Yale University Press, 1997).

57. *Chicago Defender*, January 15, 2000.

58. "Democratic Candidate Says Fitzgerald 'Betrayed' State," *Springfield Daily Herald*, January 22, 2003.

59. "Delegates Wowed by Speakers," *Emporia Gazette*, July 28, 2004.

60. "Obama's Drama and Our Dreams," *Chicago Tribune*, August 1, 2004: "At Last a Political Race Where Race Matters Less," *Financial Times*, August 16, 2004.

61. "Obama's Drama and Our Dreams."

62. "Obama Revives MLK's Dream," *Denver Post*, August 1, 2004.

63. David A. Hollinger, *Cosmopolitanism and Solidarity* (Madison: University of Wisconsin Press, 2005), 62; Lee Raiford and Renee C. Romano, *The Civil Rights Movement in American Memory* (Athens: University of Georgia Press, 2006), xvii. Two quite different and provocative reflections on the political uses of history are Richard Neustadt and Ernest R. May, *Thinking in Time: The Uses of History for Decision Makers* (New York: Free Press, 1986), and Margaret MacMillan, *Dangerous Games: The Uses and Abuses of History* (New York: Modern Library, 2009).

CHAPTER 2
OBAMA AND THE TRULY DISADVANTAGED:
THE POLITICS OF RACE AND CLASS

1. Ken Auletta, *The Underclass* (New York: Random House, 1982); Nicholas Lemann, "The Origins of the Underclass," *Atlantic* 257 (June 1986); Michael B. Katz, "The 'Underclass' as a Metaphor of Social Transformation," in Katz, ed., *The "Underclass" Debate: Views from History* (Princeton: Princeton University Press, 1993), 3–23; Herbert Gans, *The War against the Poor* (New York: Basic Books, 1995); Adolph Reed, "The Underclass as Myth and Symbol," *Radical America* 24 (1992): 21–40.

2. Obama, *Dreams from My Father*, 20–21.

3. On 1984 black turnout, see National Research Council, *A Common Destiny: Blacks and American Society* (Washington, D.C.: National Academy Press, 1989), 235–37.

4. Material in this and the next paragraph is drawn from Arnold R. Hirsch, *Making the Second Ghetto: Race and Housing in Chicago, 1940–1960* (New York: Cambridge University Press, 1983); Amanda Seligman, *Block by Block: Neighborhoods and Public Policy on Chicago's West Side* (Chicago: University of Chicago Press, 2005); Beryl Satter, *Family Properties: Race, Real Estate, and the Exploitation of Black Urban America* (New York: Metropolitan Books, 2009).

5. Liza Mundy, *Michelle: A Biography* (New York: Simon and Schuster, 2008), is the best overview of Michelle LaVaughn Robinson

Obama's life to date. On the role of civil rights organizations in opening jobs for African Americans, see Arvarh E. Strickland, *History of the Chicago Urban League* (Urbana: University of Illinois Press, 1966); Peter J. Eisinger, "Affirmative Action in Municipal Employment: The Impact of Black Political Power," *American Political Science Review* 76 (1982): 380–92; Eisinger, "The Economic Conditions of Black Employment in Municipal Bureaucracies," *American Journal of Political Science* 26 (1982): 754–71; Michael B. Katz and Mark J. Stern, *One Nation Divisible: What America Was and What It Is Becoming* (New York: Russell Sage Foundation, 2005), 91–93. On affirmative action generally, see John David Skrentny, *The Ironies of Affirmative Action* (Chicago: University of Chicago Press, 1996), and Nancy MacLean, *Freedom Is Not Enough: The Opening of the American Workplace* (Cambridge, Mass.: Harvard University Press, 2007).

6. The indispensible study of public education in Chicago is Kathryn M. Neckerman, *Schools Betrayed: Roots of Failure in Inner-City Education* (Chicago: University of Chicago Press, 2007). For data on Chicago's public schools between 1968 and 2000, see Brown University Initiative on Spatial Structures in the Social Sciences, American Communities Project, "The State of Public School Desegregation," http://www.s4.brown.edu/schoolsegregation/desegregationdata.htm.

7. Adam Green, *Selling the Race: Culture, Community, and Black Chicago, 1940–1955* (Chicago: University of Chicago Press, 2006); David Grazian, *Blue Chicago* (Chicago: University of Chicago Press, 2003); Troy Duster, "Postindustrialism and Youth Employment: African Americans as Harbingers," in Katherine McFate, Roger Lawson, and William Julius Wilson, eds., *Poverty, Inequality, and the Future of Social Policy: Western States in the New World Order* (New York: Russell Sage Foundation, 1995), 466–73.

8. Fred C. Harris, *Something Within: Religion in African American Political Activism* (New York: Oxford University Press, 2001); Mary Pattilo-McCoy, "Church Culture as a Strategy of Action in the Black Community," *American Sociological Review* 63 (1998): 767–84.

9. Rick Halpern, *Down on the Killing Floor: Black and White Workers in Chicago's Packinghouses, 1904–1954* (Urbana: University of Illinois Press, 1997); Roger Horowitz; *"Negro and White, Unite and Fight!": A Social History of Industrial Unionism in Meatpacking, 1930–90* (Urbana: University of Illinois Press, 1997); Bruce Nelson,

Divided We Stand: American Workers and the Struggle for Black Equality (Princeton: Princeton University Press, 2001).

10. Hirsch, *Making the Second Ghetto*, is the definitive history. See also Arnold R. Hirsch, "Massive Resistance in the Urban North: Trumbull Park, Chicago, 1953–1966," *Journal of American History* 82 (1995): 522–50; Seligman, *Block by Block*; James R. Ralph, Jr., *Northern Protest: Martin Luther King, Jr., Chicago, and the Civil Rights Movement* (Cambridge, Mass.: Harvard University Press, 1993); Adam Cohen and Elizabeth Taylor, *American Pharaoh. Mayor Richard J. Daley: His Battle for Chicago and the Nation* (Boston: Houghton Mifflin, 2000); and Alan B. Anderson and George W. Pickering, *Confronting the Color Line: The Broken Promise of the Civil Rights Movement in Chicago* (Athens: University of Georgia Press, 1986); Sugrue, *Sweet Land of Liberty*, 228, 237–42, 415–20, 452–54; Michael B. Katz, "Chicago School Reform as History," *Teachers College Record* 94 (1992): 56–72.

11. Mark Santow, "Saul Alinsky and the Dilemmas of Race in the Postwar City" (Ph.D. diss., University of Pennsylvania, 2000); and Sanford Horwitt, *Let Them Call Me Rebel. Saul Alinksy: His Life and Legacy* (New York: Knopf, 1989).

12. Obama, *Dreams from My Father*, 149.

13. On Chicago's deindustrialization, see, among others, David Bensman and Roberta Lynch, *Rusted Dreams: Hard Times in a Steel Community* (New York: McGraw Hill, 1987); Gregory Squires, *Chicago: Race, Class, and the Response to Urban Decline* (Philadelphia: Temple University Press, 1989); William Julius Wilson, *The Truly Disadvantaged: The Inner City, the Underclass, and Public Policy* (Chicago: University of Chicago Press, 1987).

14. "Obama's Mentor: Community Organizer Jerry Kellman Trained the Man Who Would Become President," *Illinois Issues*, March 2009. Mendell, *Obama*, 64–79; Lizza, "The Agitator"; "Service Changes People's Character," interview with Jerry Kellman, *Newsweek* online, September 5, 2008, http://www.newsweek.com/id/157424.

15. "What Makes Obama Run?" *Chicago Reader*, December 8, 1995.

16. Obama quoted in Moberg, "Obama's Community Roots."

17. "What Makes Obama Run?"

18. Sugrue, *Sweet Land of Liberty*, 356–448, 521–24; Obama, "Problems and Promise in the Inner City."

19. "Teaching Law, Testing Ideas, Obama Stood Slightly Apart," *New York Times*, July 30, 2008.

20. On the University of Chicago's role in urban renewal in Hyde Park, see Hirsch, *Making the Second Ghetto*, 135–70.

21. Craig Calhoun, ed., *Sociology in America: A History* (Chicago: University of Chicago Press, 2007), 14–16; Martin Bulmer, *The Chicago School of Sociology: Institutionalization, Diversity, and the Rise of Sociological Research* (Chicago: University of Chicago Press, 1984).

22. William Julius Wilson, *The Declining Significance of Race* (Chicago: University of Chicago Press, 1978): on politics in the 1970s, see, among others, Bruce Schulman, *The Seventies: The Great Shift in American Culture, Society, and Politics* (New York: Free Press, 2001); and Bruce Schulman and Julian Zelizer, eds., *Rightward Bound: Making America Conservative in the 1970s* (Cambridge, Mass.: Harvard University Press, 2008).

23. Stephen Steinberg, *Race Relations: A Critique* (Stanford, Calif.: Stanford University Press, 2007); and, generally, Alice M. O'Connor, *Poverty Knowledge: Social Science, Social Policy, and the Poor in Twentieth-Century U.S. History* (Princeton: Princeton University Press, 2001).

24. Obama, *Dreams from My Father*, 283, 286.

25. Wilson, *Declining Significance*, esp. 56–62.

26. Obama, "Problems and Promise in the Inner City."

27. Wilson, *The Truly Disadvantaged*; William Julius Wilson, "Public Policy Research and *The Truly Disadvantaged*," in Christopher Jencks and Paul Peterson, eds., *The Urban Underclass* (Washington, D.C.: The Brookings Institution, 1991), 460; for the full text of the Moynihan report and an overview of the debate that it generated, see Lee Rainwater and William L. Yancey, eds., *The Moynihan Report and the Politics of Controversy* (Cambridge, Mass.: MIT Press, 1967); for influential conservative views of poverty, see Charles Murray, *Losing Ground: American Social Policy, 1950–1980* (New York: Basic Books, 1984); Lawrence Mead, *The New Politics of Poverty: The Nonworking Poor in America* (New York: Basic Books, 1992); Thomas J. Sugrue, "The Impoverished Politics of Poverty," *Yale Journal of Law and the Humanities* 6 (1994): esp. 169–79. For a wide-ranging discussion of poverty politics in the twentieth century, see James T. Patterson, *America's Struggle against*

Poverty in the Twentieth Century (Cambridge, Mass.: Harvard University Press, 2000).

28. Obama, "Problems and Promise in the Inner City"; Michelle Boyd, "Reconstructing Bronzeville: Racial Nostalgia and Neighborhood Redevelopment," *Journal of Urban Affairs* 22 (2000): 107–22; "Head of Law Review Takes Aim at Other Traditions," *Philadelphia Tribune*, April 20, 1990. For Obama's views about neighborhood development in greater detail, see the interview with Barack Obama, "Hyde Park's Own Renaissance Man," *Hyde Park Herald*, July 7, 1999.

29. For alternatives, see Joe William Trotter, Jr., "Blacks in the Urban North: The 'Underclass Question,'" in Michael B. Katz, ed., *The "Underclass" Debate: Views from History* (Princeton: Princeton University Press, 1993), 55–81; Thomas J. Sugrue, *The Origins of the Urban Crisis* (Princeton: Princeton University Press, 1996), chap. 6; Douglas S. Massey and Nancy A. Denton, *American Apartheid* (Cambridge, Mass.: Harvard University Press, 1993); Reynolds Farley, "Residential Segregation of Social and Economic Groups among Blacks, 1970–1980," in Jencks and Peterson, *The Urban Underclass*, 274–98; Mary Patillo, "Sweet Mothers and Gangbangers: Managing Crime in a Black Middle-Class Neighborhood," *Social Forces* 76 (1998): 751; Richard D. Alba, John R. Logan, and Paul E. Bellair, "Living with Crime: The Implications of Racial/Ethnic Differences in Suburban Location," *Social Forces* 73 (1994): 427; and Mary Pattillo-McCoy, *Black Picket Fences: Privilege and Peril among the Black Middle Class* (Chicago: University of Chicago Press, 2000). Wilson now acknowledges the precariousness of middle-class life in the inner city. See William Julius Wilson and Richard Taub, *There Goes the Neighborhood: Racial, Ethnic, and Class Tensions in Four Chicago Neighborhoods and Their Meaning for America* (New York: Knopf, 2006), esp. 128–60.

30. "What Makes Obama Run?"; Obama, *Audacity of Hope*, 291–95, expresses his most Wilsonian understanding of public policy. Quotation from 293.

31. "A Town Meeting on Economic Insecurity," *New Ground* 45 (March–April 1996), http://www.chicagodsa.org/ngarchive/ng45.html.

32. Public Law 104-193, 22 Aug. 1996, 110 Stat. 2105; for assessments, see Michael B. Katz, *The Price of Citizenship: Redefining the American Welfare State* (New York: Metropolitan Books, 2001); Sharon Hays, *Flat Broke with Children: Women in the Age of Welfare*

Reform (New York: Oxford University Press, 2002); Jason DeParle, *American Dream: Three Women, Ten Kids, and a Nation's Drive to End Welfare* (New York: Viking, 2004); and Ellen Reese, *Backlash against Welfare Mothers: Past and Present* (Berkeley and Los Angeles: University of California Press, 2005). On its Republican origins, see "Personal Responsibility Act," in Ed Gillespie and Bob Schellhas, eds., *Contract with America* (New York: Times Books, 1994), 65–77; R. Kent Weaver, "Ending Welfare as We Know It," in Margaret Weir, ed., *The Social Divide: Political Parties and the Future of Activist Government* (Washington, D.C.: Brookings Institution, 1998), 361–416.

33. The classic work in this vein was by sociologist Theda Skocpol, *Social Policy in the United States: Future Possibilities in Historical Perspective* (Princeton: Princeton University Press, 1995), 250–74.

34. Edsall and Edsall, *Chain Reaction; Sleeper, The Closest of Strangers*; Peter Brown, *Minority Party: Why the Democrats Face Defeat in 1992 and Beyond* (Washington, D.C.: Regnery Publishers, 1991); Mickey Kaus, *The End of Equality* (New York: Basic Books, 1992); Stanley Greenberg, *Middle-Class Dreams: The Politics and Power of the New American Majority* (New York: Random House, 1995); Michael Tomasky, *Left for Dead: The Life, Death, and Possible Resurrection of Progressive Politics* (New York: Free Press, 1996); Ronald Radosh, *Divided They Fell: The Demise of the Democratic Party, 1964–1996* (New York: Free Press, 1996). For critical analyses, see Philip A. Klinkner with Rogers M. Smith, *The Unsteady March: The Rise and Decline of Racial Equality in America* (Chicago: University of Chicago Press, 1999), 303–5, 308–16; Adolph Reed, "Race and the Disruption of the New Deal Coalition," *Urban Affairs Quarterly* 27 (1991): 326–33; Felicia A. Kornbluh, "Why Gingrich? Welfare Rights and Racial Politics, 1965–1995," in Judith Jackson Fossett and Jeffrey A. Tucker, eds., *Race Consciousness: African-American Studies for the New Century* (New York: New York University Press, 1997), 193–207.

35. Kenneth S. Baer, *Reinventing Democrats: The Politics of Liberalism from Reagan to Clinton* (Lawrence: University Press of Kansas, 2000).

36. Wilson, *The Truly Disadvantaged*, 140–64; Wilson elaborated on this argument in a later book: *The Bridge over the Racial Divide: Rising Inequality and Coalition Politics* (Berkeley and Los Angeles: University of California Press, 1999).

37. David T. Ellwood and Mary Jo Bane, *Welfare Realities: From Rhetoric to Reform* (Cambridge, Mass.: Harvard University Press, 1994), offers insight into the liberal social science that shaped Clinton's thinking about welfare reform.

38. Interview (1996) quoted in "Teaching Law, Testing Ideas, Obama Stood Slightly Apart," *New York Times*, July 30, 2008; "Obama Pledges to Be Hardest Working Senator in Springfield," *Chicago Weekend*, January 16, 1997; Barack Obama, "Help Needed to Change Springfield," *Hyde Park Herald*, February 19, 1997; "State Taxes Block Road Off Welfare," *Chicago Tribune*, April 10, 1999; Obama, *Audacity of Hope*, 42–44, 213–14, 303–7 (quotation, 303).

39. For discussions of these issues, see Michael Dawson, *Black Visions: The Roots of Contemporary African-American Political Ideologies* (Chicago: University of Chicago Press, 2001); Melissa Victoria Harris-Lacewell, *Barbershops, Bibles, and BET: Everyday Talk and Black Political Thought* (Princeton: Princeton University Press, 2004), esp. chaps. 2–3.

40. Mary Pattillo, *Black on the Block: The Politics of Race and Class in the City* (Chicago: University of Chicago Press, 2007); Evelyn Brooks Higginbotham, *Righteous Discontent: The Women's Movement in the Black Baptist Church, 1880–1920* (Cambridge, Mass.: Harvard University Press, 1993); Kevin K. Gaines, *Uplifting the Race: Black Leadership, Politics, and Culture in the Twentieth Century* (Chapel Hill: University of North Carolina Press, 1996).

41. Jeremiah A. Wright, Jr., "Doing Black Theology in the Black Church," in Linda E. Thomas, ed., *Living Stones in the Household of God: The Legacy and Future of Black Theology* (Minneapolis, Minn.: Fortress Press, 2004) , 13–23, offers a detailed description of his church's ministries. For other accounts of Wright's ministry and sermons, see "Ministers Reflect on Role Black Church Has Played in America," *Chicago Weekend*, February 16, 1997; "Black Churches Must Fight AIDS," *Los Angeles Sentinel*, December 3, 1998; Jeremiah Wright, Jr., "A Luta Continua," *Philadelphia Tribune*, December 3, 2006; Emily Udell, "Keeping the Faith," *In These Times*, February 28, 2005; "Rev. Jeremiah Wright's Words," *Chicago Tribune*, March 26, 2008.

42. "Youth Get Paid for Academic Excellence," *Philadelphia Tribune*, June 14, 1994.

43. "Empowering the African American Male," *Michigan Citizen*, March 11, 1995; Wright, "Doing Black Theology," 20.

44. Obama, "A More Perfect Union." On black religion and politics, see Barbara Dianne Savage, *Your Spirits Walk beside Us: The Politics of Black Religion* (Cambridge, Mass.: Harvard University Press, 2008).

45. "Barack and Michelle Obama Begin Their Storied Journey," 60.

46. Obama, "Selma Voting Rights March Commemoration"; "Remarks of Senator Barack Obama: The Great Need of the Hour," Atlanta, Georgia, January 20, 2008, http://www.barackobama.com/2008/01/20/remarks_of_senator_barack_obam_40.php; "Remarks of Senator Barack Obama: Apostolic Church of God," June 15, 2008, http://www.barackobama.com/2008/06/15/remarks_of_senator_barack_obam_78.php; "Remarks by the President to the NAACP Centennial Convention," July 16, 2009, http://www.whitehouse.gov/the_press_office/Remarks-by-the-President-to-the-NAACP-Centennial-Convention-07/16/2009/.

47. "Remarks of Senator Barack Obama: Apostolic Church of God"; "Soul Survivor: Bobby Rush," *Chicago Tribune*, November 16, 2003; Bill Cosby and Alvin Poussaint, *Come on People* (Chicago: William Nelson, 2007), 2, 3, 221; see also Michael Eric Dyson, *Is Bill Cosby Right?* (New York: Perseus Books, 2005); Thomas J. Sugrue, "Hearts and Minds," *Nation*, May 12, 2008.

48. Obama, *Audacity of Hope*, 301.

49. Obama, *Audacity of Hope*, 15.

Chapter III
"A More Perfect Union"?
The Burden of Race in Obama's America

1. "The Grant Park Rally," *Chicago Tribune*, November 5, 2008; Obama, "A More Perfect Union."

2. See Chuck Todd and Sheldon Gawiser, *How Barack Obama Won: A State-by-State Guide to the Historic 2008 Presidential Election* (New York: Vintage Books, 2009); "Election Night in Hyde Park," *Chicago Maroon*, November 4, 2008. See Charles Franklin, "Demographic Groups and Votes, 2008," November 10, 2008, http://www.pollster.com/blogs/demographic_groups_and_votes_2.php, esp. table 3.

3. Night for Dancing, Not Trouble, in the Streets," *Chicago Sun-Times*, November 5, 2008; "Barack Obama Sweeps to Victory," *Chicago Defender*, November 5–11, 2008; "Daley Celebrates a Peaceful Rally," *Chicago Sun-Times*, November 6, 2008; "'A Long Time Coming': Obama's Neighbors Celebrate His Victory," *Hyde Park Herald*, November 12, 2008.

4. For data on segregation in Chicago, see James Lewis, Michael Maley, Paul Kleppner, and Ruth Ann Tobias, *Race and Residence in the Chicago Metropolitan Area, 1980–2000* (Chicago: Institute for Metropolitan Affairs, 2002); Chicago Urban League, *Still Separate, Still Unequal: Race, Place, Policy, and the State of Black Chicago* (Chicago: Chicago Urban League, 2006).

5. *Chicago in Focus: A Profile from Census 2000* (Washington, D.C.: The Brookings Institution, 2006), 23–28; Street, *Racial Oppression*, 168.

6. Herbert J. Gans, "The Possibility of a New Racial Hierarchy in the Twenty-First Century United States," in Michèle Lamont, ed. *The Cultural Territories of Race* (Chicago: University of Chicago Press and Russell Sage Foundation, 1999), 371–90; David A. Hollinger, *Postethnic America: Beyond Multiculturalism* (New York: Basic Books, 1995); see "Symposium on the Latin Americanization of Race Relations in the United States," *Race and Society* 5 (2002): 1–114.

7. On housing discrimination and public policy, see, among others, Kenneth T. Jackson, *Crabgrass Frontier: The Suburbanization of the United States* (New York: Oxford University Press, 1985); Steven Grant Meyer, *As Long as They Don't Move Next Door: Segregation and Racial Conflict in American Neighborhoods* (Lanham, Md.: Rowman and Littlefield, 2000); Massey and Denton, *American Apartheid*, 192–200; Eduardo Bonilla-Silva, *Racism without Racists: Color-Blind Racism and the Persistence of Racial Inequality in the United States* (Lanham, Md.: Rowman and Littlefield, 2003). For a related use of this concept, see Ford, *The Race Card*.

8. Wilson and Taub, *There Goes the Neighborhood*.

9. *Chicago in Focus*, 22.

10. Lawrence D. Bobo, Melvin L. Oliver, James H. Johnson, Jr., and Abel Valenzuela, Jr., *Prismatic Metropolis: Inequality in Los Angeles* (New York: Russell Sage Foundation, 1999); Camille Zubrinsky Charles, *Won't You Be My Neighbor? Race, Class, and Residence in Los Angeles* (New York: Russell Sage Foundation, 2006).

11. Richard Alba and Victor Nee, *Remaking the American Mainstream: Assimilation and Contemporary Immigration* (Cambridge, Mass.: Harvard University Press, 2003), offers the most comprehensive overview of these patterns.

12. Reynolds Farley, "Racial Identities in 2000," in Joel Perlmann and Mary C. Waters, eds., *The New Race Question* (New York: Russell Sage Foundation. 2002); Sonya M. Tafoya, Hans Johnson, and Laura E. Hill, "Who Chooses to Choose Two?" in Reynolds Farley and John Haaga, eds., *The American People: Census 2000* (New York: Russell Sage Foundation, 2005), 332–51; Jennifer Lee and Frank D. Bean, "Reinventing the Color Line: Immigration and America's New Racial/Ethnic Divide," *Social Forces* 86 (2007): 561–86.

13. Min Zhou, "Are Asian Americans Becoming 'White'?" *Contexts* 3, no. 1 (2004): 29–37.

14. See Michael Jones-Correa, "Reshaping the American Dream: Immigrants, Ethnic Minorities, and the Politics of the New Suburbs," in Kevin M. Kruse and Thomas J. Sugrue, eds., *The New Suburban History* (Chicago: University of Chicago Press, 2006), 183–204; Audrey Singer, "The Rise of the New Immigrant Gateways," Brookings Institution, Living Cities Census Series, February 2004, http://www.brookings.edu/urban/pubs/20040301_gateways.pdf; William H. Frey, "Diversity Spreads Out: Metropolitan Shifts in Hispanic, Asian, and Black Populations since 2000," Brookings Institution, Living Cities Census Series, March 2006, http://www.frey-demographer.org/reports/R-2006-1_DiversitySpreadsOut.pdf.

15. John Logan, Reynolds Farley, and Brian Stults, "Segregation of Minorities in the Metropolis: Two Decades of Change," *Demography* 41 (2004): 1–22. John Iceland, Daniel H. Weinberg, and Erika Steinmetz, U.S. Census Bureau, Series CENSR-3, *Racial and Ethnic Segregation in the United States, 1980–2000, Census 2000 Special Reports* (Washington, D.C.: U.S. Government Printing Office, 2002); Massey and Denton, *American Apartheid.*

16. For summaries of these patterns, see, in general, Kenneth T. Jackson, "Race, Ethnicity, and Real Estate Appraisal: The Home Owners Loan Corporation and the Federal Housing Administration," *Journal of Urban History* 6 (1980): 419–52; Arnold R. Hirsch, "With or Without Jim Crow: Black Residential Segregation in the United States," in Arnold R. Hirsch and Raymond A. Mohl, eds., *Urban Policy in Twentieth-*

Century America (New Brunswick, N.J.: Rutgers University Press, 1993), 65–99; and Massey and Denton, *American Apartheid*.

17. Diana Pearce, "Gatekeepers and Homeseekers: Institutionalized Patterns in Racial Steering," *Social Problems* 26 (1979): 325–42; Massey and Denton, *American Apartheid*, 98–104; John Yinger, *Housing Discrimination Study: Incidence of Discrimination and Variation in Discriminatory Behavior* (Washington, D.C.: U.S. Department of Housing and Urban Development, 1991) and Yinger, *Closed Doors, Opportunities Lost: The Continuing Costs of Housing Discrimination* (New York: Russell Sage Foundation, 1995); Michael Fix and Raymond J. Struyk, eds., *Clear and Convincing Evidence: Measurement of Discrimination in America* (Washington, D.C.: Urban Institute Press, 1993).

18. "'No Child' Law Is Not Closing Racial Gap," *New York Times*, April 29, 2009.

19. Davison M. Douglas, *Reading, Writing, and Race: The Desegregation of the Charlotte Schools* (Chapel Hill: University of North Carolina Press, 1995); Matthew Lassiter, "'Socioeconomic Integration' in the Suburbs: From Reactionary Populism to Class Fairness in Metropolitan Charlotte," in Kruse and Sugrue, *New Suburban History*, 140–43; *Capacchione v. Charlotte-Mecklenburg Schools* 57 F. Supp. 2d 228 (1999); *Parents Involved in Community Schools v. Seattle School District No. 1*, 551 U.S. 701 (2007).

20. Massey and Denton, *American Apartheid*, 4–87, table 4.1; John Iceland, Cicely Sharpe, and Erika Steinmetz, "Class Differences in African American Residential Patterns in US Metropolitan Areas: 1990–2000," *Social Science Research* 34 (2005): 252–66.

21. Kathryn Neckerman and Joleen Kirschenmann, "We'd Love to Hire Them, but . . . : The Meaning of Race for Employers," in Jencks and Peterson, *The Urban Underclass*, 203–32; Marianne Bertrand and Sendhil Mullainathan, "Are Emily and Greg More Employable than Lakisha and Jamal? A Field Experiment on Labor Market Discrimination," *American Economic Review* 94 (2004): 991–1013; Chris Tilly et al., "Space as a Signal: How Employers Perceive Neighborhoods in Four Metropolitan Labor Markets," in Alice O'Connor, Chris Tilly, and Lawrence Bobo, eds., *Urban Inequality: Evidence from Four Cities* (New York: Russell Sage Foundation, 2001), 304–39; Keith R. Ihlanfeldt and David L. Sjoquist, "The Spatial Mismatch Hypothesis: A Review of

Recent Studies and Their Implications for Welfare Reform," *Housing Policy Debate* 9 (1998): 849–92.

22. United States Census Bureau, *Income, Earnings, and Poverty from the 2006 American Community Survey* (Washington, D.C.: U.S Census Bureau, 2007).

23. United States Census Bureau, "Net Worth and Asset Ownership of Households: 1998 and 2000," *Current Population Reports: Household Studies*, May 2003, 12. On the black-white gap, see Thomas M. Shapiro, *The Hidden Cost of Being African American: How Wealth Perpetuates Inequality* (New York, 2004); Dalton Conley, *Being Black, Living in the Red: Race, Wealth, and Social Policy in America* (Berkeley and Los Angeles: University of California Press, 1999); and Melvin L. Oliver and Thomas M. Shapiro, *Black Wealth, White Wealth: A New Perspective on Racial Inequality* (New York: Routledge, 1997). Darrick Hamilton and William Darity, Jr., "Race, Wealth, and Intergenerational Poverty," *American Prospect On-Line*, August 19, 2009, http://www.prospect.org/cs/articles?article=race_wealth_and_intergenerational_poverty.

24. Algernon Austin, "Subprime Mortgages Are Nearly Double for Hispanics and African Americans," Economic Policy Institute, June 11, 2008, http://www.epi.org/economic_snapshots/entry/webfeatures_snapshots_20080611/; Andrew Jakabovics and Jeff Chapman, "Unequal Opportunity Lenders? Analyzing Racial Disparities in Big Banks' Higher Priced Lending," Center for American Progress, September 2009, http://www.americanprogress.org/issues/2009/09/pdf/tarp_report.pdf; Jennifer Wheary, Tatjana Meschede, and Thomas M. Shapiro, "The Downside before the Downturn: Declining Economic Security among Middle-Class African Americans and Latinos, 2000–2006," Brandeis University, Institute on Assets and Social Policy and Demos, n.d., http://www.demos.org/pubs/bat_5.pdf.

25. National Center for *Health Statistics, Health, United States 2006*, table 27, www.cdc.gov/nchs/data/hus/hus06.pdf.

26. National Center for *Health Statistics, Health, United States 2006*, Table 27, www.cdc.gov/nchs/data/hus/hus06.pdf; William J. Bennett et al., *Body Count: Moral Poverty and How to Win America's War against Crime and Drugs* (New York: Simon and Schuster, 1996), 66; Devah Pager, "The Mark of a Criminal Record," *American Journal of Sociology* 108 (2003): 937–75; Becky Pettit and Bruce Western, "Mass

Imprisonment and the Life Course: Race and Class Inequality in U.S. Incarceration," *American Sociological Review* 69 (2004): 151–69.

27. Satta Sarmah, "Is Obama Black Enough?" *Columbia Journalism Review*, February 15, 2007, http://www.cjr.org/politics/is_obama_black_enough.php; "Blacks Shift to Obama, Poll Finds," *Washington Post*, February 28, 2007; Gary Younge, "Is Obama Black Enough?" *Guardian*, March 1, 2007; "Who Is Ready for Change?" *Washington Post*, January 24, 2008; "Will Obama Pay for Bitter Flap?" *Time*, April 14, 2008.

28. "Obama Routs Clinton in South Carolina," *San Francisco Chronicle*, January 27, 2008; "Seeking Unity, Obama Feels Pull of Racial Divide," *New York Times*, February 12, 2008; "Newsletter's Obama Illustration Denounced," *Los Angeles Times*, October 17, 2008; "G.O.P. Receives Obama Parody to Mixed Reviews," *New York Times*, December 27, 2008.

29. Andrew Gelman and John Sides, "Stories and Stats: The Truth about Obama's Victory Wasn't in the Papers," *Boston Review*, September/October 2009.

30. Pew Research Center, *Optimism about Black Progress Declines: A Social and Demographic Trends Report* (Washington, D.C.: Pew Center, 2007), 54, available at http://pewsocialtrends.org/assets/pdf/Race.pdf.

31. For a thoughtful reflection on these issues, see Benjamin DeMott, *The Trouble with Friendship: Why Americans Can't Think Straight about Race* (New Haven: Yale University Press, 1998).

32. Jennifer L. Hochschild, *Facing Up to the American Dream: Race, Class, and the Soul of the Nation* (Princeton: Princeton University Press, 1995), esp. chap. 3, offers the most detailed analysis to date of surveys of black and white public opinion on discrimination and economic success.

33. Orlando Patterson, "Obama's America: Equality," *Democracy: A Journal of Ideas*, Winter 2009, 9.

34. The impact of diversity is the subject of intense scholarly and popular debates. William Bowen and Derek Bok, *The Shape of the River: Long-Term Consequences of Considering Race in College and University Admissions* (Princeton: Princeton University Press, 1998), argue that the diversification of higher education has created a cadre of minority community leaders committed to civic betterment, and has expanded the pool of talent available to corporations, firms, and

nonprofits. Walter Benn Michaels, *The Trouble with Diversity: How We Learned to Love Identity and Ignore Inequality* (New York: Henry Holt, 2006), argues that a commitment to diversity reinforces class privilege, creating a multicultural elite, while leaving the fundamental economic causes of inequality untouched. Both have elements of truth. Bok and Bowen draw from extensive survey research to make a case that minority elites are more likely to provide resources and support to the disadvantaged than are their white counterparts. But they overstate the societal benefits of a diverse elite. Michaels is right that diversity efforts themselves do not necessarily remedy inequality. But he paints with too broad a brush all civil rights initiatives as exclusive of economic justice, ignoring the constitutive nature of racial and economic inequality and the long history of efforts by grassroots activists and policymakers to address the disadvantages of race and class simultaneously.

35. The number of books and articles on affirmative action, most of them polemical, is vast. Representative and influential conservative critics of affirmative action include Stephan Thernstrom and Abigail Thernstrom, *America in Black and White: One Nation Indivisible* (New York: Simon and Schuster, 1997); Herman Belz, *Equality Transformed: A Quarter-Century of Affirmative Action* (New Brunswick, N.J.: Transaction Publishers, 1991); Terry Eastland, *Ending Affirmative Action: The Case for Colorblind Justice* (New York: Basic Books, 1996). For two excellent overviews that situate conservative arguments in their cultural and political context while avoiding ideological cant, see Jennifer L. Hochschild, "Affirmative Action as Culture War," in Lamont, ed., *Cultural Territories of Race*, 343–68, and John David Skrentny, *The Ironies of Affirmative Action* (Chicago: University of Chicago Press, 1996).

36. See, for example, Gitlin, *Twilight of Common Dreams*; Richard Kahlenberg, *The Remedy: Class, Race, and Affirmative Action* (New York: Basic Books, 1996); and Jim Sleeper, *Liberal Racism* (New York: Viking Press, 1997).

37. Obama, *Audacity of Hope*, 293.

38. Gunnar Myrdal, *An American Dilemma* (New York: Harper, 1944), 5.

39. Pew Research Center, *Optimism about Black Progress Declines*, 30.

40. *Parents Involved in Community Schools v. Seattle School District*

No. 1, 551 U.S. 701 (2007). The most thorough effort to account for the costs of affirmative action on whites is in Bowen and Bok, *Shape of the River.*

41. *Regents of the University of California v. Bakke*, 438 U.S. 265 (1978).

42. Remarks by the President to the NAACP Centennial Convention, July 16, 2009, http://www.whitehouse.gov/the_press_office/Remarks-by-the-President-to-the-NAACP-Centennial-Convention-07/16/2009/.

43. Obama, "A More Perfect Union"; "Obama's 'Typical White Person' Makes Waves," *Philadelphia Inquirer*, March 22, 2008; "Obama Aide Concedes 'Dollar Bill' Remark Referred to His Race," *ABC News*, August 1, 2008, http://abcnews.go.com/GMA/Politics/story?id=5495348&page=1; "Companies Remove Ads from Beck Program on Fox News," *New York Times*, August 13, 2009; "Race Issue Deflected, Now as in Campaign: Obama Maintains Criticism Is about Policy Differences," *Washington Post*, September 17, 2009. Examples of racial caricatures of Obama are abundant online.

44. Some commentators have argued that Obama should exhort whites to personal responsibility, just as he does blacks. See Tim Wise, *Between Barack and a Hard Place: Racism and White Denial in the Age of Obama* (San Francisco: City Lights Books, 2009), 111–49.

45. MacLean, *Freedom Is Not Enough*; Chandler Davidson and Bernard Grofman, eds., *Quiet Revolution in the South: The Impact of the Voting Rights Act, 1965–1990* (Princeton: Princeton University Press, 1994); Massey and Denton, *American Apartheid*, 192–200; Christopher Bonastia, *Knocking on the Door: The Federal Attempt to Desegregate the Suburbs* (Princeton: Princeton University Press, 2006).

46. U.S. Department of Justice, Office of the Inspector General and Office of Professional Responsibility, *An Investigation of Allegations of Politicized Hiring and Other Improper Personnel Actions in the Civil Rights Division*, July 2, 2008, http://www.usdoj.gov/oig/special/s0901/final.pdf. See also "Justice Department to Recharge Civil Rights Division," *New York Times*, August 31, 2009.

47. Barack Obama, "Remarks of Senator Barack Obama: Howard University Convocation," Washington, D.C., September 28, 2007, http://www.barackobama.com/2007/09/28/remarks_of_senator_barack_obam_26.php; see also Jeffrey Rosen, "Race to the Top," *New*

Republic, April 22, 2009; "Westchester Adds Housing to Desegregation Pact," *New York Times*, August 11, 2008.

48. As of November 2009, 15.7 percent of blacks, 13.1 percent of Hispanics, and 9.5 percent of whites were unemployed. "Blacks Hit Hard by Economy's Punch," *Washington Post*, November 24, 2009; Heidi Hartmann, "Gender Implications of the Financial Crisis in the United States," April 22, 2009, http://www.boell.org/downloads/Heidi_Hartmann_Paper_Final.pdf; "NAACP Prods Obama on Job Losses," *New York Times*, November 16, 2009.

49. Daniel Gitterman, Joanne Spetz, and Matthew Fellowes, "The Other Side of the Ledger: Federal Health Spending in Metropolitan Economies," Brookings Institution Metropolitan Policy Program, September 2004, http://www.brook.edu/metro/pubs/20040917_gitterman.htm.

50. Obama, "A More Perfect Union"; see also "Prepared Remarks of President Barack Obama: Back to School Event," Arlington, Virginia, September 8, 2009, http://www.whitehouse.gov/mediaresources/PreparedSchoolRemarks/.

51. The best summary of integration's positive effects on educational outcomes is Jennifer Hochschild and Nathan Skovronick, *The American Dream and the Public Schools* (New York: Oxford University Press, 2003). The scholarship on charter schools is polemical and contentious. For a favorable interpretation of the Harlem Children's Zone, see Paul Tough, *Whatever It Takes: Geoffrey Canada's Quest to Change Harlem and America* (New York: Houghton, Mifflin, Harcourt, 2008).

52. On localism, see Jon C. Teaford, *City and Suburb: The Political Fragmentation of Metropolitan America* (Baltimore, Md.: Johns Hopkins University Press, 1979); Thomas J. Sugrue, "All Politics Is Local: The Persistence of Localism in Twentieth-Century America," in Meg Jacobs, William J. Novak, and Julian Zelizer, eds., *The Democratic Experiment: New Directions in American Political History* (Princeton: Princeton University Press, 2003), 301–26; Lizabeth Cohen, *A Consumer's Republic: The Politics of Mass Consumption in Postwar America* (New York: Knopf, 2003), chap. 5; and Richard Thompson Ford, "The Boundaries of Race: Political Geography in Legal Analysis," in Kimberle Crenshaw et al., eds., *Critical Race Theory: The Key Writings That Formed the Movement* (New York: The New Press, 1996), 449–64.